T0320963

THE JOURNAL OF
CORPORATE
CITIZENSHIP

Issue 54
June 2014

Theme Issue: **Storytelling: Beyond the Academic Article – Using Fiction, Art and Literary Techniques to Communicate**

Edited by
Nick Barter, Griffith Business School, Griffith University, Australia
Helen Tregidga, AUT University, Faculty of Business and Law, New Zealand

Greenleaf
PUBLISHING

print ISSN 1470-5001   *online* ISSN 2051-4700

THE JOURNAL OF CORPORATE CITIZENSHIP

General Editor Malcolm McIntosh,
Asia-Pacific Centre for Sustainable Enterprise, Griffith Business School, Australia

Regional Editor North America: Professor Sandra Waddock, Boston College, Carroll School of Management, USA

Publisher Rebecca Macklin, Greenleaf Publishing, UK **Assistant Publisher** Anna Comerford, Greenleaf Publishing, UK

Production Editor Dean Bargh, Greenleaf Publishing, UK

CORRESPONDENCE

The Journal of Corporate Citizenship encourages response from its readers to any of the issues raised in the journal. All correspondence is welcomed and should be sent to the General Editor c/o Greenleaf Publishing, Aizlewood's Mill, Nursery St, Sheffield S3 8GG, UK; jcc@greenleaf-publishing.com.

All content should be submitted via **online submission**. For more information see the journal homepage at www.greenleaf-publishing.com/jcc.

Books to be considered for review should be marked for the attention of the Book Review Editor c/o Greenleaf Publishing, Aizlewood's Mill, Nursery St, Sheffield S3 8GG, UK; jcc@greenleaf-publishing.com.

• All articles published in *The Journal of Corporate Citizenship* are assessed by an external panel of business professionals, consultants and academics.

• *The Journal of Corporate Citizenship* is indexed with and included in: **Cabells, EBSCO, ProQuest, Gale, ABDC** and **Journalseek.net**. It is monitored by 'Political Science and Government Abstracts' and 'Sociological Abstracts'.

SUBSCRIPTION RATES

The Journal of Corporate Citizenship is a quarterly journal, appearing in March, June, September and December of each year. Cheques should be made payable to Greenleaf Publishing and sent to the address below.

Annual online subscription
Individuals: £80.00/€112.50/US$150.00
Organizations: £540.00/€650.00/US$850.00

Annual print and online subscription
Individuals: £90.00/€120.00/US$160.00
Organizations: £550.00/€672.50/US$860.00

Annual print subscription
Individuals: £80.00/€112.50/US$150.00
Organizations: £180.00/€240.00/US$320.00

The Journal of Corporate Citizenship
Greenleaf Publishing Ltd, Aizlewood Business Centre, Aizlewood's Mill, Nursery Street, Sheffield S3 8GG, UK
Tel: +44 (0)114 282 3475   Fax: +44 (0)114 282 3476   Email: jcc@greenleaf-publishing.com.
Or order from our website: www.greenleaf-publishing.com/jcc.

FSC
www.fsc.org
MIX
Paper from responsible sources
FSC® C013604

Printed in the UK on environmentally friendly, acid-free paper from managed forests by CPI Group (UK) Ltd, Croydon

Editorial

Writing with Heart, Body, Soul, Brain and Mindfulness

Issue 54 *June 2014*

Malcolm McIntosh

General Editor, Journal of Corporate Citizenship

Fiction, more than any other written form, explains and expands life. Biology, of course, also explains life; so do biography and biochemistry and biophysics and biomechanics and biopsychology. But all the biosciences yield to fiction. Novels tell us the most truth about life: what it is, how we live it, what it might be for, how we enjoy and value it, how it goes wrong, and how we lose it. Novels speak to and from the mind, the heart, the eye, the genitals, the skin; the conscious and the unconscious.

> Julian Barnes *Through The Window* (2011) Preface. 2011 Booker Prize winner.

THE *JOURNAL OF CORPORATE CITIZENSHIP* knows that its readers take their discourse seriously, but that they also like a good yarn or story. Many of them are involved in writing the stories of their companies and presenting them as sustainability or social reports. All reports and all scholarly pieces are narratives of a sort, each choosing which evidence suits and each having some sense of beginning, middle and end.

We all aim to be communicative, and in the world of business and management we also aim to be convincing.

In the world of academia we try to survive the vicissitudes of university life and the depredations of conformity, and so it also is in corporate life. This journal has tended, as its title suggests, to be interested in the 'corporate' but what a merry tale we weave around our personal and professional lives as we step in and out of various daily values portals. How could we tell our stories differently, and how could companies tell their stories differently if we didn't all conform to a narrow model of corporatism, managerialism and neoliberal economics?

How might the world look if we genuinely wanted to encompass and share all stakeholders' viewpoints: if we truly wanted conscious capitalism? Or is it that most stakeholder engagement involves conforming to that early definition of stakeholder engagement: 'people, issues and organisations that impact on the originating organisation's performance'? For example here's a quotation from one of the 2013 longlisted Booker Prize novels. It's by Colm Tóibín and it tells the story not of Jesus (an heroic male) but of his mother, Mary. She is watching him being nailed to the cross:

He was a boy I had given birth to and he was more defenceless now than he had been then ... In those days if I had even dreamed that I would see him bloody, and the crowd around filled with zeal that he should be bloodied more, I would have cried out that day and that cry would have come from that part of me that is the core of me. The rest of me is merely flesh and blood and bone ... For the nailing part, we stood back ...

Colm Tóibín The Testament of Mary (2013) Penguin

An enlightenment, or even post-modern, perspective tell us that there is no certainty—'God is dead' Nietzsche told us back in 1882—but humanism and learning has stepped into that space such that we can embrace the multiple endings of John Fowles' 1965 novel *The Magus* and his annotated novel *The French Lieutenant's Woman* in 1969 and Tóibín's post-patriarchal perspective of Christ's crucifixion and resurrection.

We may pride ourselves on our postmodernism and transdisciplinary approach to research but academic scholars are still fearful of not sign-posting the modernist accumulation of knowledge, as if referencing previous scholars legitimises what's currently on the page. And so it is to a certain extent with the pieces in this *JCC* special edition.

This edition of the journal, edited by Helen Tregidga and Nick Barter, called for discussions on how we tell stories and how we might tell different stories if we were allowed. This isn't the moment, and we don't have the space here now, to write about the patriarchal nature of some of our organisations and institutions and the colonial nature of many of our trading arrangements but a number of the articles in this collection do just that, overtly and covertly—through stories. Can I thank Helen and Nick and all the contributors for a fascinating set of papers.

Malcolm McIntosh
June 2014
Queensland, Australia

Guest Editorial

Storytelling
Beyond the Academic Article: Using Fiction, Art and Literary Techniques to Communicate[*]

Nick Barter
Griffith University, Australia

Helen Tregidga
AUT University, New Zealand

In this guest editorial we have two aims. First, to outline the background to, and motivation for, this special issue, which called for contributions that went beyond the academic article and used fiction and other literary techniques to communicate; and second, to introduce the papers and briefly outline their contribution. We conclude the editorial with some reflections on the preparation of this issue and a call for academics to embrace the uncertainty associated with communicating their ideas in novel forms.

T HAS BEEN ARGUED THAT narrative is a key device through which humans attempt 'to find meaning in an overwhelmingly crowded and disordered chronological reality' (Cronon, 1992, p. 1349). Or perhaps, more simply, storytelling (narrative) is key to how we understand the world around us (Weick, 1995). In turn narratives are important to how we understand organisations and are enrolled to realise organisational strategies (Barry and Elmes, 1997; Fenton and Langley, 2011; Guber, 2007; Guerin, 2003). Narratives saturate our lives and as long as there is intent with human speech there will be narrative and rhetoric (Norreklit 2003). Thus in everything we do we have a protagonist in a context who, through time, moves towards an outcome. In these narratives, the

---

* Acknowledgements unfortunately also suffer with a rhetorical razor and as such are likely to leave out someone important; to that person we apologise. However, rhetorical razors aside we would like to thank Professor Malcolm McIntosh, the General Editor of the *Journal of Corporate Citizenship* for being open to and supporting this special issue. We would also like to thank the publishing team at Greenleaf, in particular Claire Jackson and Rebecca Macklin for their advice and guidance. In addition we thank those who supported this issue by acting as reviewers, the contributors for their papers and finally those who reviewed this editorial and provided valuable insights and suggestions.

outcome tends to be either enlightened or tragic, and as such the plotline leading to the outcome is either ascending or descending (Cronon, 1992), fearful or hopeful (Pesquex 2009, p. 231). As authors of our narratives, behind them all is the unavoidable understanding that they are a construction and thus suffer from an inevitable refraction whereby the author(s) of the narrative have, either knowingly or unknowingly, applied a 'rhetorical razor...that defines included and excluded, relevant and irrelevant, empowered and disempowered' (Cronon, 1992, p. 1349). This inescapable rhetorical razor inevitably silences some while giving voice to others. Indeed this editorial and the articles within this special issue, no matter what the author(s) intentions, suffer the fate of the rhetorical razor. Further, a reader always brings their context to a narrative, and in doing so, a raft of actors that may otherwise be unknown to the author(s) can make a claim regarding inclusion or exclusion. As such every story has innumerable interpretations.

An understanding that narratives saturate our world was a stimulus for the call for papers that has resulted in this special issue. There is a narrative about how the guest editors met, where and when, and how, through conversation, they serendipitously identified a mutual interest in communicating beyond the academic article; however that narrative is superfluous and silenced. In short, a key motivation behind this call for papers was an understanding that many academics have become locked to a particular style of narrative privileged by the academic system and that style, while useful, is perhaps limiting.

It has been claimed that the modern mind is 'haunted by the belief that the only meaningful concepts are those capable of mathematical elucidation' (Gladwin, Newburry and Reiskin, 1997, p. 248; see also, Cummings 2005; Boisot and McKelvey, 2010). Further this is a type of rationalism that 'supports the doctrine that facts are separate from values...and that truth is a function of objective reality' (Gladwin et al., 1997, pp. 248). Arguably academic articles and textbooks defer to this rationality via, for example, the metaphor of 'textbook operation'. This is a metaphor that implies operating to a set of agreed upon and regulated procedures (Crawford, 2003), that are conducted in a bubble of ahistorical, decontextualised truth (Cummings and Bridgman, 2011), where the individual and their values and understanding are removed from the sphere of concern. In removing the protagonist from the narrative, the narrative moves from being a story about a researcher and what they found to being an article and/or textbook that is simply a 'delivery system of facts' (Apple and Christian-Smith, 1991 p. 1; see also Pinnegar and Daynes, 2007)—an objective non-story. In short, the story and the non-story are separated (Cronon, 1992), as in a 'rational world' knowledge is not gained from a subjective story, rather it is gained from an objective non-story. However, while an objective, decontextualised, dehumanised research narrative may appeal to current truth claims, the difficulty is that another truth is lost; that of the researcher and their values. Thus the story is lost to the non-story and to cycle back to the beginning of this editorial, this may limit understanding (Weick, 1995).

Within this context, as guest editors we approached *The Journal of Corporate Citizenship* to establish whether they would be interested in our proposal of a special issue of 'academic' papers that embraced fiction, art and other literary techniques in order to communicate to an audience. *The Journal of Corporate Citizenship* has a history of embracing innovative submissions that might include photographs, poetry and paintings. Further, its remit is bringing ideas to practitioners and academics alike. Consequently moving beyond the standard academic article was, we found, consistent with the journal's aims and they accepted our proposal.

The original call for papers was issued in the final quarter of 2012. That call opened with a quote from Bateson (2002) that outlined how even a computer might think in terms of storytelling. In response to that call we received numerous enquiries and submissions. Thus our assumption, and hope, that our colleagues are creative and looking for alternatives in presenting their work was realised. The submissions received came from across the world and from a variety of disciplines, thus the interest in moving beyond the academic article appears not to be a localised phenomenon. Through the usual process of double blind peer review the articles that constitute this issue were identified. They are introduced in the next section of this editorial. As will be seen, the papers accepted reflect the diversity of submissions received. While we suspect each reader will interpret the papers in different ways, with some resonating positively and others not so, what is common to all the papers is a desire to engage the reader in a novel, interesting and memorable way. After introducing the articles we close with some comments on the challenges of editing this special issue, some opportunities for the future.

In this issue

There are seven papers in this issue; the first is a re-telling of a well-known fairy tale, the second discusses the use of art, the third, fourth and fifth use fictional stories to explain the consequences of theory and/or research findings, the sixth discusses how a napkin can help tackle institutional racism and the final paper offers a poem to problematise the move towards Open Access.

The first paper by Simons (2014) explores the role and power of sacred stories by re-telling a well-known fairy tale from an alternative perspective. In so doing Simons (2014) seeks to highlight how, in societies and organisations, there are voices that are marginalised. In the paper Simons (2014) retells the *Little Red Riding Hood* fairy tale from the big bad wolf's perspective, a voice that has been silenced in the modern day version of the story. Through the re-telling of the story Simons (2014) attempts to make it possible to understand the actions of, and identify with, the wolf—something not easily done in the common and familiar telling of the story. As such, Simons (2014) uses the fairy tale to expose and question power relations. Using this platform, Simons (2014) argues that within the social sciences and organisations sacred stories are causes of exclusion and marginalisation. She posits that it is important to pay attention to silent voices, consider things from different perspectives, and look for meanings which are not necessarily those which we take for granted.

The second paper discusses individuals' commitment to sustainable outcomes and how it can be fostered via the use of art workshops and individuals painting their understandings of sustainability. This practice is termed by the authors, Ivanaj, Poldner and Shrivastava, as aesthetic practice pedagogy. They argue the practice deepens understandings of sustainability and sustainable enterprise by connecting our hands, heart and heads—our feelings, our practices and our cognition. Thus they argue that aesthetic practice pedagogy is able to 'evoke deep personal, emotional understanding and commitment to action'. The article discusses the art-based workshops and how these workshops aim to integrate art and science in a transdisciplinary way to provide more holistic understandings of sustainability by participants. Through analysing structured feedback from workshop participants, the authors argue that aesthetic practice pedagogy has both value and power. In doing so, they provide a structure for a workshop which others may choose to utilise or develop.

The third paper in this issue was motivated by an observation that higher education students generally do not engage with academic material and in not doing so they hinder their ability to develop a critical understanding of theories. To counter this lack of critical engagement, Barter and Houghton present a fictional story set in a non-specific future. The story is informed by theories and is titled 'Is This OK?' The theories that inform the story include, but are not limited to, the concept of natural capitalism and how humans are a negotiation, a process. Specifically the story focuses on the temporal understanding of humanity, companies offering solutions rather than products or services, and the valuing (monetarisation) of ecosystem services. Through presenting theories and concepts in a fictional story and by applying the theories and concepts to an extreme within it, a platform for exposition and discussion is provided. Reflecting on their own experiences and anecdotal observations when utilising the story within the classroom context, this paper provides insights, not only into how fictional stories grounded in theory can be used pedagogically, but also, as an exemplar which readers may choose to utilise themselves.

The fourth and fifth papers in this issue relate to the university context and more specifically academics and academic life. The fourth paper by Harris, Ravenswood and Myers has at its core a fictional story that is used to consolidate and present the results of a study, with academics, on the vagaries of the academic promotion process within a university. More specifically, Harris *et al.* examine the promotion process by paying particular attention to gender and the advancement of women. What makes the paper particularly novel is that the findings are presented under the title of the 'The Quest Games'. 'The Quest Games' brings forward shades of a gladiatorial contest and is written without reference to the academic context or gender. This fiction enables the story to be relevant to a wider audience. This contribution by Harris *et al.* not only provides insight into the area of career advancement (in particular within the university setting) but also is an example of how narrative inquiry and fictional storytelling can be used to present findings in a novel and engaging way.

Similarly, the fifth paper creates a fictional story to present its findings from research with academics. In this paper, Ryan and Guthrie explore the increasing corporatisation of the university sector. Drawing on findings from a longitudinal study based on interviews with academics from Australian Graduate Business Schools, they develop 'The Story of Bill'— a hypothetical academic—to relay the changes that the university sector has undergone in recent years. Bill is used to represent the 'voice' of all the academics in the study. Using the story Ryan and Guthrie provide insight into the life of an academic in a period of significant institutional change. Thus, as with the previous paper, this paper highlights how storytelling can be used to communicate research findings in novel and insightful ways.

The sixth paper in this special issue documents how a researcher used a paper napkin to communicate and disseminate her findings regarding institutional racism to a non-academic audience. In this paper, Came and Humphries, two self-identified activist researchers, discuss institutional racism within the context of public health and health policy in Aotearoa/New Zealand. The paper discusses how to make the invisible visible and in so doing disseminate findings succinctly, hence the napkin. Came and Humphries argue that the napkin is a particularly powerful dissemination device because it is an everyday object which is often disposed of in an unthinking manner. While obviously important to an academic engaged in activism, Came and Humphries' contribution addresses a topic which is important for many academics—how to communicate research to a non-academic audience.

The issue is completed with a paper from Mannay who utilises her own experiences and a poem to reflect on the changing requirements of research dissemination, specifically Open Access. The paper reflects on ways in which the move towards Open Access realises concerns regarding ethics, obligations and integrity. Through the poem and supporting commentary Mannay raises the complexity of the changing research dissemination landscape and argues for the need to 'consider all stakeholders in the march towards progressive dissemination' and Open Access.

Close

The seven papers in this special issue, we believe, offer the reader something different from that which they might typically expect. In particular through their use of fiction, art and poetry the papers are challenging what might typically be expected as the form of an academic article. Further, each of the papers has a message that is attempting to challenge convention and what is typically 'acceptable'. These challenges include the identifying of silent voices, the linking of our hands, hearts and heads via art, a poem, a napkin to communicate, the life of an average academic, stories of gladiatorial combat for promotion or a man's day in a non-specific future. This mix of challenge in both form and message contributes, in our view, to the ability of the papers to advance understanding. Further it reinforces how an innovative approach to conveying the message can advance debate; in short getting beyond the academic article is valuable.

Having made the call, had the papers reviewed and consolidated into this special issue, two key things we have learned as guest editors is to be bolder and to embrace the uncertainty. With regards to being bolder, on reflection we think we could have pushed for further creativity in the papers and would do so if asked to do another special issue. As can be seen the papers are a form of hybrid in that they mix their creativity with conventional academic writing. This was perhaps partly the result of our call for papers which included the requirement of a statement of the academic foundations for the submission as well as the use of the 'traditional' review process. Hence if we were to make this call again we would perhaps be bolder in moving away from a hybrid model and allowing contributors to fully embrace their creative potential: albeit the limits of a journal's printing format and structure are still likely to put some boundaries around that creativity. In terms of embracing the uncertainty, this is more a lesson for us as editors. Perhaps like all special issue editors we had robust debate about advice for authors and which submissions to include and exclude. From our perspective these debates were more difficult because of the nature of the submissions—and, perhaps like many editors and guest editors, we relied on reviewer comments in informing our decisions. As discussed, the submissions embrace the story and as such move away from convention. This made us less sure of our ground as we found ourselves debating, in the broadest terms, the aesthetics of a submission. Thus as editors we felt more uncertain than we expected, as the difficulty of aesthetics is that beauty is always in the eye of the beholder. In summary, having learned what we have now learned from editing this special issue, I think in the future we would be not only bolder, but also more willing to embrace uncertainty—uncertainty itself being a result of a challenge to our conventions, our paradigms.

References

Apple, M., and Christian-Smith, L. (1991) 'The politics of the textbook'. In M. Apple & L. Christian-Smith (Eds.), *The Politics of the Textbook*, (pp. 1-22), London: Routledge.

Barry, D., and Elmes, M. (1997) 'Strategy Retold: Toward a Narrative View of Strategic Discourse' *Academy of Management Review*, 22(2), 429-452.

Bateson, G. (2002) *Mind and Nature: A Necessary Unity*, Hampton Press: Creskill, NJ.

Boisot, M. and McKelvey, B. (2010) 'Integrating Modernist and Postmodernist Perspectives on Organizations: A Complexity Science Bridge.' *Academy of Management Review*, 35(3), 415–433.

Crawford, K. (2003) 'The role and purpose of textbooks', *International Journal of Historical Learning, Teaching and Research*, 3(2), 5-11.

Cronon, W. (1992) 'A place for stories: Nature, history and narrative', *The Journal of American History*, 78(4), 1347-1376.

Cummings, S. (2005). *Recreating Strategy*. London: Sage.

Cummings, S., and Bridgman, T. (2011) 'The relevant past: Why the history of management should be critical for our future', *Academy of Management Learning & Education*, 10(1), 77-93.

Fenton, C., and Langley, A. (2011) 'Strategy as Practice and the Narrative Turn', *Organization Studies*, 32(9): 1171-1196.

Gladwin, T. N., Newbury, W. E., and Reiskin, E. D. (1997) 'Why is the northern elite mind biased against community, the environment and a sustainable future?' In M.H. Bazerman, D.M. Messick, A.E. Tenbrunsel and K.A. Wade-Benzoni (Eds.), *Environment, Ethics and Behavior: The Psychology of Environmental Valuation and Degradation*. San Francisco: The New Lexington Press.

Guber, P. (2007) 'The four truths of the storyteller' *Harvard Business Review* 85 (12): 52-59.

Guerin, B. (2003) 'Language use as social strategy: a review and an analytic framework for the social sciences' *Review of General Psychology* 7 (3): 251-98.

Norreklit, H. (2003) 'The Balanced Scorecard: what is the score? A rhetorical analysis of the balanced scorecard' *Accounting, Organizations and Society* 28: 591-619.

Pesquex, Y. (2009) 'Sustainable development: a vague and ambiguous theory' *Society and Business Review* 4 (3): 231-245.

Pinnegar, S.and Daynes, J.G. (2007) 'Locating narrative inquiry historically: Thematics in the turn to narrative', In D.J. Clandinin (Ed.), *Handbook of Narrative Inquiry: Mapping a Methodology*. Thousand Oaks: Sage Publications.

Weick, K. (1995) *Sensemaking in Organisations*, Sage: USA.

Dr **Nick Barter** is a senior lecturer in strategy and sustainability and is the MBA director at Griffith. Prior to Griffith he spent 5 years at the University of St Andrews in the UK. His current research includes metaphors and conceptions of the environment.

✉ Griffith Business School, Griffith University, Room 4.26, Building S07, Southbank Campus, PO Box 3370, South Brisbane, QLD 4101, Australia

🖥 n.barter@griffith.edu.au

Dr **Helen Tregidga** is a Senior Lecturer in Accounting in the Faculty of Business and Law at AUT University, New Zealand. Her research interests are primarily related to the interface of business, society and the natural environment.

✉ AUT University, Faculty of Business and Law, AUT City Campus, Private Bag 92006, Auckland 1142, New Zealand

🖥 helen.tregidga@aut.ac.nz

Sacred Stories and Silent Voices

What The Big Bad Wolf Can Teach Us*

Ilja Simons

NHTV Breda University of Applied Sciences, the Netherlands

This paper explores the power of stories and how they can give voice to the unheard. The first part of the paper consists of a story. The fairy tale of *Little Red Riding Hood* has been rewritten from the wolf's perspective. The wolf has been a silent voice in the fairy tale for a long time. Writing the story from his perspective makes it easier to understand his actions and identify with him. The second part of the paper is an explanatory section, which describes how the story of *Little Red Riding Hood* can be seen as a metaphor for discourse and hidden power relations. Often in organisations, in communities, and in societies there are voices present that are not being heard. It is hard to pay attention to these voices because they are so difficult to hear, even when they speak. Other voices are louder, more familiar or just the majority. It is argued that 'sacred stories' are an important cause of exclusion and, especially in an organisation that wants to be a learning organisation, we should pay attention to silent voices instead of overruling them. Silent voices have a different perspective, which might help discover organisational blind spots. But in order to look beyond our sacred stories, we need to look for other means than the obvious. Fiction could be one of those means, being a silent voice within the dominant discourses of social science itself.

- Storytelling
- Fairy tales
- Narratives
- Sacred stories
- Silent voices
- Discourse

Ilja Simons is a Lecturer in the Academy for Leisure at the NHTV Breda, University of Applied Sciences in Breda, The Netherlands. She holds a Master's degree in Sociology and specialises in cross-cultural understanding. Her research interests include storytelling, identities, power relations and silent voices within the context of leisure and tourism. More specifically, her current work examines cultural events as social practices in which group and individual identities are created and maintained.

NHTV Breda, University of Applied Sciences, Breda, the Netherlands

Simons.i@nhtv.nl

* I am very grateful for the cooperation in the NHTV research groups of Vincent Platenkamp (Cross Cultural Understanding) and Moniek Hover (Storytelling), which helped me to develop this line of thinking. Furthermore, thanks are due to the two anonymous reviewers for their helpful and detailed comments, as well as to Annet Ghering and Brian Wheeler for their attentive reading. Finally, thanks to Helen Tregidga and Nick Barter for their help with editing this article.

The story of the fearful wolf

Once upon a time there was a little wolf without a father or a mother. His father had left a long time ago, and the little wolf had missed him ever since. His father was a strong wolf, the biggest of them all. With him by his side the little wolf was never afraid. But now, without his dad, he was a bit scared, and that was why the other wolves made fun of him. And not just the wolves, even the tiniest bunnies and squirrels would laugh at him. Walking through the woods he would hear them whisper and giggle. 'Look, there's that fearful wolf', 'A bit of a chicken, that wolf isn't he?'

Sometimes the wolf would see his father. When he passed a ditch or a pond, or just a puddle, he would suddenly see his father's big head appear out of nowhere. Surprised, his father would stare at him, looking more fierce and frightening than ever. A real big bad wolf, not a coward like he was. 'Hi', they would say, simultaneously, but then, after a few seconds, his father would disappear again in the ripples of the water. Seeing his father made the fearful wolf happy. For a while he forgot how fearful he was, and he growled at the bunny rabbits that quickly ran away. That would teach them!

One day the wolf was wandering through the woods when suddenly he heard a voice. As he was afraid, he hid behind a tree. A human appeared. A small human, but still he preferred to keep a distance. But the human came closer and closer to the tree. When the wolf looked more closely, he saw a little girl wearing a red hood. Despite the wolf's efforts to hide, the girl came closer still and finally she spotted the wolf behind the tree. 'Ahum', the wolf cleared his throat and spoke in his nicest voice:

'Good day little girl, where are you going so early?'

'I am going to see my grandmother, to bring her some cookies and wine', the girl said, 'but my mummy told me not to stray from the path, or I might meet the big bad wolf'.

'But have you not strayed from the path right now?' the wolf answered. If only that girl had listened to her mother, he would not have had to hide, he thought, and he would not have had to converse with a human, something he did not fancy at all.

'I saw such beautiful flowers I wanted to pick', the girl said. The wolf was hungry and looked with a stray eye at the cookies in the girl's basket. Would she give him one, he wondered? But he was too fearful to ask.

'Do you know how to get to grandmother's cottage?' the girl asked. 'That way', the wolf responded quickly. He pointed in a random direction, without thinking, hoping the girl would disappear soon. 'Oh thank you very much', the girl said, and she left. The wolf watched her go and he realised he had sent her even further into the woods. That way it would take her a long time to reach her grandmother's cottage. He wanted to call out to her, but he was too fearful.

With an empty stomach he went back to his wandering, thinking about the little girl's cookies. She had been quite a nice little girl. If he had dared to ask, she probably would have given him a cookie, he thought. That gave him an idea. The wolf started to run to grandmother's cottage. There he would wait for the girl and ask for a cookie after all. Proud of his courage, he ran through the woods, no longer afraid and howled with joy. Soon he reached grandmother's cottage. Now he just had to wait for the girl. He stood in front of grandmother's door. He waited and waited, but the girl did not show. When after a while he sat down against the door, he heard a voice: 'Is that you Little Red Riding Hood? Lift the latch and the door will open'. It was grandmother.

Well, the wolf thought over-confidently, the girl had been so nice, maybe her grand-mother is even nicer. She might just give me the cookie and then I don't have to wait for the girl anymore. So he lifted the latch. The door opened and he jumped inside. Immediately the old lady started screaming and shouting. 'Ssssshush', the wolf said, 'the hunter might hear us! Silence now, I just wanted to eat something.' But that last remark only made grandmother scream even louder.

The wolf became more fearful than he had ever been, and in a panic, he leaped across the room and swallowed the old lady whole. A deadly silence followed.

'Oh no', the wolf moaned, 'What have I done? Any minute now, Little Red Riding Hood will appear with her cookies and she will expect grandmother to be lying in her bed. When she sees me, she will surely understand what I have done. And how should I explain that?'

Quickly the wolf changed into grandmother's night gown, put on her cap and crawled into her bed. There he waited for Little Red Riding Hood. He did not have to wait for long. After a short while there was a knock on the door and he heard a voice: 'Hello grandmother, it is Little Red Riding Hood. I am bringing you cookies and some wine'.

'Just lift the latch and the door will open' said the wolf.

Little Red Riding Hood approached the bed and the wolf noticed her shock right away. His heart started to pound. Would she realise what he had done?

'Grandmother, what large ears you have' she said. Relieved the wolf answered: 'The better to hear you with.'

'But grandmother, what great eyes you have', the girl continued. 'The better to see you with', said the wolf, his heart pounding in his throat.

'What large hands you have?'

'The better to hold you with', the wolf said nervously. This way Little Red Riding Hood would find out any minute that it was not grandmother but him lying in the bed. All his courage had disappeared and his fearfulness had returned more fiercely than ever. If only he had never met this girl.

But Little Red Riding Hood had no intention of stopping the questioning and spoke: 'But grandmother, what a terribly large mouth you have!' The fearful wolf howled out of desperation and he only saw one way out. 'The better to devour you with!' he shouted, bewildered, and with one big bite he swallowed up Little Red Riding Hood as well.

There he was, the fearful wolf. Sitting in grandmother's nightgown. Next to the bed stood the basket with cookies, but after what had happed, he had lost his appetite. Grandmother and Little Red Riding Hood weighed heavily on his stomach and not knowing what to do, he fell asleep. He had an unpleasant dream, about a hunter who opened up his stomach which allowed grandmother and Little Red Riding Hood to jump out. That would be nice for them, but of course this was only a dream. The dream continued with the hunter filling his stomach with rocks. What a nasty dream, he thought, feeling the cold rocks in his belly. The horror continued when grandmother turned up next to him with a needle and started to sew his stomach together. Aarrrgh! In vain he tried to wake up from this terrible nightmare. Finally the wolf awoke and he decided to leave the cottage as quickly as he could, before anyone would find out what had happened. His stomach hurt and he had trouble walking. A terrible thirst came *over him and he had to drink before he could walk on. Not far from grandmother's cottage, he came to a well. In it, all of a sudden, he discovered his father's face. 'Hi', they said simultaneously, and this time his father did not disappear in the ripples of the water. Instead he pulled his son towards him. The wolf bent deeper and deeper until his paw touched his father's. A deep sense of happiness came over the wolf, and while the cool water drenched his skin, all the fearfulness left him. He sank deeper and deeper into a close, warm embrace with his father. From now on, he would never let go of his father's paw. Ever.*

The End

Explanation

THIS IS AN EXPLANATION OF why I felt the need to alter the fairy tale of *Little Red Riding Hood*. It might, for some, seem odd or disrespectful to change a classic story and to make up an extra part. So, why did I feel the need to write the story from the wolf's perspective and why did I not just enjoy the story the way it was?

Little Red Riding Hood

Little Red Riding Hood has become one of the sacred stories of our times. Ever since the Grimm brothers documented it, it has been part of our shared heritage. Reading the story over and over again to my children I began to realise that the strict distinction between good and bad, the morals of not talking to strangers, and the punishment of the wolf did not really fit into these postmodern times. My children, however, were fascinated by the story and made me read it over and over again. The first few times they asked questions about the other characters. And especially the intention of the wolf to eat Little Red Riding Hood was hard for my two-year-old daughter to accept. She insisted for almost a year that the wolf really just wanted to eat the cookies that Little Red Riding Hood was carrying. But despite their first objections, after reading the story more than 20 times, they had become so familiar with it that they stopped questioning and copied the story as I read it to them. Based on the pictures in the storybook, they could 'read' the story by themselves and they corrected me if I did not tell the story correctly. I was struck by the change I observed in my children. I preferred the questioning, the open mindedness and the creativity they had shown before. But the repetition of the story took that away. Now they just wanted to hear the same thing over and over again. It made me think of the socialisation process as a whole and I wondered what other sacred stories we believe in, and never question. I realised that, just like in the story of *Little Red Riding Hood*, these other sacred stories are always told from the same perspective, hold rigid categories, and there are always characters whose voices are silent or silenced. That is when I decided to write the story of the fearful wolf. Not to read it to my children, but to read it to adults.

Exploring the fairy tale of *Little Red Riding Hood* a bit more I found that the Grimm brothers, whose version is so popular nowadays, based their version on the fairy tale of Perrault (Zipes, 1995; Hover, 2013). Perrault's version of 1697 is far crueller. A naive Little Red Riding Hood is held responsible for the wolf's behaviour and ends up raped and killed. Originally, when the story was told before an audience, interaction was possible between the storyteller and the listeners and questions could be asked in order to make the story suit the listeners better. The story was not frozen in time, but it was adapted to the needs of the audience (Hover, 2013). So originally there was room for questions about the wolf's motives and other voices could be included. I even found evidence of the wolf having a voice. In an earlier play by Tieck, *Leben und Tod des kleinen Rotkäppchens*, the wolf talks about his own life. He explains that he used to be a guard dog, who met a wild female wolf who he married. Unfortunately, his wife was killed by peasants and the wolf wanted to take revenge by eating Little Red Riding Hood (Hover, 2013: 67). When the Grimm brothers wrote their version of the story they altered it to make it more suitable for children. Unnecessary cruelty as well as explicit sexual references were taken out; in Perrault's version, Little Red Riding Hood undresses and climbs into bed with the wolf. The fairy tale was altered to fit the middle class values of that time, and the wolf lost his voice. Nowadays, we feel that the fairy tale is a part of our shared intangible heritage, and we do not question it anymore. In that sense fairy tales are perfect metaphors for the background assumptions that we have, that make our world understandable, but at the same time keep us from understanding others or gaining insights that are not in line with our discourse.

Science and fiction

In post-modern literature, it is not uncommon to question traditional heroes by choosing another's perspective (Bertens, 2004). An example is the book *Foe* by Coetzee (1986), who introduces a third person in the story of Robinson Crusoe and Friday. This other voice, Susan Barton, has a completely different story, but she lacks the language to share it. Furthermore, we can see a trend of traditional fairy tales being modernised for different purposes. *Little Red Riding Hood* is an inspiration for many authors (Zipes, 1993). Gwen Strauss (1993) gives the wolf a poetic voice in her poem *The Waiting Wolf*. However, it is not common to use fairy tales or fiction as part of academic writing in social sciences. Even I believed that *Little Red Riding Hood* was something to read to my children as a bedtime story, and I thought it had no place in academic writing. But while I was lecturing about narratives and silent voices, the two worlds blended together.

Nowadays, a narrative approach has been widely accepted in the social sciences. Many speak of a narrative turn (Watson, 2009, 2011; Michelson 2012). Narratives play an important role, both as a research method, and as an explanation of behaviour (Kohler Riessman, 2008). For example, it is well accepted that (self)stories form identities and that these storied identities shape action (Bruner, 1987; Gergen and Gergen, 1988; Presser, 2012).

But this so-called narrative turn does not necessarily include the use of fiction or related genres (Hackley, 2007; Watson, 2011). Watson (2011: 396) claims this is a result of a 'deeply felt need for research to be grounded in an empirical reality of something that *really happened*'. A difficulty lies in the difference in rhetoric between fiction and social science. This leads to expectations on the part of the reader and responsibilities for the author (Richardson and St Pierre, 2005; Watson, 2011). Writing something that is fiction and social science at the same time will not meet these expectations, and therefore runs the risk of being dismissed. But however complicated relations between fiction and science may be, there are several ways in which they interrelate (De Cock and Land, 2006; Watson 2011).

De Cock and Land (2006: 519) distinguish three modes of engagement with literature. The approach I use in this article would fit what they call 'literature as a pedagogical tool to explicate theory, for the purpose of illustration of themes and ideas or as a resource for critique'. I believe fiction can be an important means to challenge pre-existing assumptions because it persuades people to identify with the characters. Graaf *et al.* (2012) show in an experiment how perspective influences identification. The participants in their research were asked to read a fictional story that was told from two different characters' perspectives—both with opposing goals. This way they illustrate how identification can be a mechanism of narrative persuasion (Graaf *et al.*, 2012). In addition to this, I believe fairy tales are suitable for discussing sensitive issues, or taboos, because they form a safe environment which is not 'real' or too close to the listener.

The big bad wolf as offender

When writing the story of the fearful wolf, I took the perspective of the wolf as an offender. Giving him a voice makes it possible to understand his actions better and identify with him. He becomes more 'human' and he has emotions of his own: he misses his father, he has a bad self-image, he looks strong, he does not recognise himself in the mirror, he is afraid to talk to humans, he is hungry, he likes cookies and so on.

What about offenders in our society? Do we want to hear their voices? Do we feel they have a right to be heard or is the fact that they are offenders a reason to silence them? One reason why we prefer not to listen to offenders' stories is the doubts we have about offenders telling the truth. Goffman (1971) points out that we have difficulties believing offenders' stories because of the incentives they face for portraying themselves in a certain way. This is part of our narrative about offenders as being bad people. Popular television shows often depict criminal suspects as lying and untrustworthy, in order to avoid sanctions (Presser, 2009). Criminologists have equally questioned how authentic offender narratives can be (Presser, 2009). Despite this discussion about authenticity, offender narratives are commonly used in criminology. Youngs and Carter (2009) derived four themes from offender narratives: Adventure, Irony, Quest and Tragedy. Katz

(1988) also discovered common plots in crimes and points out that the offender acts according to the possibilities of the plot. Besides discovering common plots and criminal story lines, giving offenders a voice can even prevent recidivism. Stevens (2012) writes about offenders staying away from crime by reframing their self-narratives and reconstructing their identities.

Sometimes offenders are turned into bad creatures by the media. An example of this occurred in the Netherlands, when a sweet sixteen party, announced on Facebook, got out of hand when, unintentionally, thousands of people were invited. They all went to the village of Haren with riots as a result (Commissie Haren, 2013). The offenders were immediately accused in the media. According to the newspapers, the riot police had never experienced such violence (Telegraaf, 2012). After a while, when things calmed down, it turned out that most of the offenders were teenagers who had never been in contact with the police before, and most of whom had been terrified. The picture of the offenders changed again after they were given a voice. They were given the opportunity to share their perspective, unlike the wolf in the fairy tale.

Sacred stories in our society

So what are the sacred stories in our society and which groups do they silence? Sacred stories are perhaps perceived to be too nice to alter. Sometimes they are rooted in history and people identify with them. Consequently, they do not want them to be changed and they are oblivious to the exclusions inherent in them. Or even more powerfully, people can be unaware of sacred stories even existing, while at the same time being influenced by them and accepting them.

An example is the post-colonialist story of orientalism (Said, 1978). The myth of orientalism creates a clear distinction between east and west, which silences the voices from the east, which are seen as irrational, sensual and primitive. A pretty picture in the eyes of the dominant west, but it forces people into the role of the other and it silences their voices. The same, it could be argued, applies to other indigenous peoples all over the world. By describing them as primitive and exotic, they are called on to preserve an authenticity that never existed, except in the minds of those that made up the story (Said, 1978; Hollinshead, 1998).

Another example of a sacred story is the pioneering myth which celebrates values like perseverance and bravery. The story of European settlers 'taming the wild frontier' still appeals to people, whereas at the same time it portrays indigenous peoples as savages. The sacred untouchable stories, told from a European perspective, have silenced people on various continents. In Australia, for example, even today, when incidents occur in which Aborigines are the offenders they are referred to as 'savages' and 'animals' on blogs on the internet (Youtube, 2009). When in 2010, Bob Geldof sharply criticised the treatment of Aborigines, he was strongly attacked on several blogs and called a hypocrite because of his own wealth (*Herald Sun*, 2010). However, it can take an outsider's perspective to see a different picture. Historian Timothy Bottoms called the treatment of Aborigines 'a conspiracy of silence'. He said 'that a foreigner like Sir Bob Geldof has the nerve to identify that "Australia has exiled indigenous

Australians from the nation" is not an effrontery, but an insight that we should have recognised ages ago' (Global Voices Online, 2010).

The same thing occurred to me when I worked in Zimbabwe in 2001. I criticised a white Zimbabwean friend of mine for treating his local workers in a, from my perspective, racist way. He was shocked. Who was I, not born in the country, to criticise him? I felt confused, did I not know enough about the context? He told me the story of his forefathers, how they had had to struggle, and how they had built this country. Compared to them he did not perceive himself to be racist at all. I realised that being an outsider made it easier to see how his workers were silenced within the story. According to his story, which only started when his forefathers had arrived in the country, the locals were the ones who needed help, and he was offering it. He was convinced he did his best, but he identified with and wished to hold on to the heroic colonial story. Around that time, President Mugabe started to create and communicate his own story, based on independence and freedom, which turned the white farmers into offenders who had to be silenced. Silencing people in such a way, with most of the silencers not even aware of it, can inevitably lead to problems and, often, conflict. As in the fairy tale of *Little Red Riding Hood*, we are now at a stage where some of the silenced voices have turned into offenders, whom we might feel have lost their voices because of their actions. And we sometimes fail to realise that it is the other way around. The moral of the story of *Little Red Riding Hood* is to not stray, not talk to strangers, especially not to wolves. In these days this does not apply anymore. We should talk to today's wolves and involve them.

The silencing of groups and individuals is inseparably linked with power. Some may believe that silent voices are the people who do not speak, but I argue that even when silent voices speak we cannot hear what they say. Simpson and Lewis (2005) make a distinction between the surface act of speaking and being heard and a deeper level of the power of silence. They describe how 'discursive practices eliminate certain issues from arenas of speech and sound' (Simpson and Lewis, 2005: 1253). There is simply no room for voices that are outside the main discourse. Issues that challenge the existing power relations have no place in existing discussions. And in order for some to be powerful and privileged, they must suppress and silence other meanings (Gabriel *et al.*, 2000; Simpson and Lewis, 2005). As Foucault (1976, cited in Simpson and Lewis, 2005: 1261) pointed out: 'Silence constitutes discourse and can be an agent of power in its own right. The unsaid can thus be illustrative of power being articulated'. Osler and Zhu (2011: 232) argue that 'untold' stories should be told and then retold, to 'examine historical wrongs; identify current oppressions; challenge dominant discourses'. Cederberg (2013) adds to this discussion that public discourses can constrain personal narratives. This has to be taken into account when studying inequalities. She shows how public discourses frame migrant narratives and normalise unequal power relations. She shows that marginal voices are not necessarily counter-hegemonic, but they sometimes reproduce the public discourse (Cederberg, 2013). This shows how powerful a dominant discourse can be. I believe that all communication means, including fiction, are allowed and should be encouraged to discover voices that are silenced. Perhaps fiction is even a perfect illustration, because it still is a silent voice itself within the dominant discourses of social science.

Sacred stories in organisations

To illustrate the relevance of all this for organisational practices, I will include an example from my daily practice as a lecturer which shows how involving other perspectives can shake loose hidden background assumptions (Platenkamp, 2007; Mainil *et al.*, 2010). This can cause sacred stories, in this case a story linked to orientalism (Said, 1978), to start to crumble. I teach in an international classroom in which different nationalities are present. This makes it possible to explore alternative interpretations of stories and experiences (Bruner, 1996). In one of my classes a Chinese girl participated. One day, in a discussion about tourism and authenticity, she told a story about wedding ceremonies in her home area in China, for which tourists were invited when they were visiting the temple. Tourists were always pleasantly surprised by the invitation. The class was charmed by the story and started to ask questions when, after a while, the Chinese girl added to the story that the weddings were not real. They were staged for the tourists. The Western students in the class were shocked and told her that they did not think that this was right. But our Chinese classmate was surprised at their reaction and did not see it as a problem at all: everybody involved was happy, she explained. This was an opportunity for the class to see a different perspective, though for most students, it was hard to be open to it. For them staging a wedding was unthinkable and they preferred the idea that a 'nice' Chinese couple would invite tourists into their lives. The students had read about staged authenticity (Cohen, 1988) before, but this discussion made them aware of their own assumptions. When the Chinese girl asked them if they would invite strangers to their wedding she made the other students see the Chinese as similar to them, instead of seeing them as others. The abstract 'local Chinese people' turned into people like their class mate—and like them.

Identifying sacred stories and silent voices is not just relevant in society in general and in educational practices, but it is crucial for organisational learning as well. Several authors have shown that stories contribute to sense making in organisations (Boje, 1991; Weick, 1995; Czarniawska, 1998). By sharing and interpreting stories, individuals try to understand organisational practices (Boyce, 1997; Czarniawska, 1998; Gabriel 2000; Soins and Scheytt, 2006; Fenton and Langley, 2011). Humphreys and Brown (2008, quoted in Fenton and Langley, 2011: 1176) even state that 'organisations literally are the narratives...which maintain and objectify reality'. So if narratives play such a big role in organisations, it is worth examining how sacred stories affect organisations and which voices are silenced.

Sole and Wilson (2002) identify some traps of knowledge sharing stories in organisations: seductiveness, single point of view and static-ness. All these traps relate to the sacredness of stories. In addition to this, Fenton and Langley (2011) point out how an overarching narrative marginalises other narratives. An example of this can be found in the article by Simpson and Lewis (2005) about gender in organisations, who argue that the dominant (male) discourse of enterprise and entrepreneurialism silences (female) meanings. Another very convincing example is given by Geiger and Antonacopoulou (2009). In their article about narratives and organisational dynamics, they demonstrate how persistent a dominant narrative can be. In their analysis they show how an organisation in crisis does not pay attention to deviating counter narratives, while holding on to a shared story about customer intimacy. The counter narratives could help solve the problem of the organisation, but they are overlooked. The authors show how a web of narratives has the potential to construct 'unquestioned self-legitimising truths', which result in blind spots for the organisation (Geiger and Antonacopoulou, 2009: 412). Furthermore, their analysis shows that the silencing of other voices is not necessarily a deliberate act of dominance, but it happens as a side-effect of narrative construction.

Conclusion

In summary, we can conclude that organisations which hold on to sacred stories may be limiting the scope for organisational learning and change. Including silent voices, on the other hand, may not only enhance justice for marginalised groups and individuals, but may also be beneficial to majority groups. In order to look beyond our sacred stories, and to reveal hidden power relations, we need to look for other means than the obvious. I believe fiction and fairy tales are examples of such means. The story of the fearful wolf invites and encourages people to look for the sacred stories in their lives. It is time to hear the wolf again, to allow him to speak, and to regard him as a valuable source of knowledge.

References

Bertens, H. (2004) *The idea of the postmodern: A history*. London: Routledge.

Boje, D. (1991) 'The storytelling organization: A study of performance in an office-supply firm', *Administration Science Quarterly*, 36.1: 106-126.

Boyce, M.E. (1997) 'Organizational story and storytelling: A critical review', *Journal of Organizational Change Management*, 9.5: 5-26.

Bruner, J.S. (1987) 'Life as narrative', *Social Research*, 54: 11-32.

Bruner, J.S. (1996) *The culture of education*. Cambridge: Harvard University Press.

Cederberg, M. (2014) 'Public Discourses and Migrant Stories of Integration and Inequality: Language and Power in Biographical Narratives', *Sociology*, 48.1: 133-149.

Coetzee, J.M. (1986) *Foe*. New York: Viking Press.

Cohen, E. (1988) 'Authenticity and commoditization in tourism', *Annals of Tourism Research*, 15.3: 371-386.

Commissie Haren (2013) *Commissie project X Haren presenteert eindrapportage*. Available at: www.commisieharen.nl (Accessed: 25 March 2013).

Czarniawska, B. (1998) *A narrative approach to organization studies*. London: Sage.

De Cock, C. and Land, C. (2006) 'Organization/literature: exploring the seam', *Organization Studies*, 27.4: 517-535.

Fenton, C. and Langley, A. (2011) 'Strategy as Practice and the Narrative Turn', *Organization Studies*, 32.9: 1171–1196.

Gabriel, Y. (2000) *Storytelling in organizations: Facts, fictions and fantasies*. Oxford, UK: Oxford University Press.

Gabriel, Y., Fineman, S. and Sims, D. (2000) *Organizing and organizations*. London: Sage.

Geiger, D. and Antonacopoulou, E. (2009) 'Narratives and Organizational Dynamics: exploring Blind Spots and Organizational Inertia', *The Journal of Applied Behavioral Science*, 45.3: 411-436.

Gergen, K.J. and Gergen, M.M. (1988) 'Narrative and the Self as Relationship', in Berkowitz, L. (ed.) *Advances in Experimental Social Psychology*, 21: 17–56. San Diego, CA: Academic Press.

Global Voices Online (2010) *Australia: Bob Geldof Rouses Aussie Rich*. Available at: www.globalvoicesonline.org/2010/05/22/australia-bob-geldof-rouses-aussie-rich (Accessed 25 March 2013).

Goffman, E. (1971) *Relations in Public: Microstudies of the Public Order*. New York: Basic Books.

Graaf, de, A. Hoeken, H., Sanders, J. and Beentjes, J.W.J. (2012) 'Identification as a Mechanism of Narrative Persuasion', *Communication Research*, 39.6: 802–823.

Hackley, C. (2007) 'Auto-ethnographic consumer research and creative non-fiction: Exploring connections and contrasts from a literary perspective', *Qualitative Market Research: An International Journal*, 10.1: 98–108.

Herald Sun (2010) 'Sir Bob Geldof slams Australia's "absurd" treatment of Aborigines', www.heraldsun.com.au/entertainment/sir-bob-geldof-says-hits-australia-is-economically-stupid/story-e6frf96x-1225868605242. (Accessed 25 March 2012).

Hollinshead, K. (1998) 'Tourism, hybridity and ambiguity: The relevance of Bhabha's "third space" cultures', *Journal of Leisure Research*, 30.1: 121-156.

Hover, M. (2013) *De Efteling als verteller van sprookjes*. PhD thesis. Tilburg University, The Netherlands.

Katz, J. (1988) *Seductions of Crime: The Moral and Sensual Attractions of Doing Evil*. New York: Basic Books.

Kohler Riessman, C. (2008) *Narrative Methods for the Human Sciences*. London: Sage Publications.

Mainil, T., Platenkamp, V. and Meulemans, H. (2010) 'Diving into the contexts of in-between worlds: worldmaking in medical tourism', *Tourism analysis*, 15.6: 743-754.

Michelson, E. (2012) 'If the Self Is a Text, What Genre Is It? Structure and Ideology in Narratives of Adult Learning', *Adult Education Quarterly*, 63.3: 199-214.

Osler, A. and Zhu, J.(2011) 'Narratives in teaching and research for justice and human rights', *Education, Citizenship and Social Justice*, 6.3: 223-235.

Platenkamp, V. (2007) *Contexts in tourism and leisure studies: a cross-cultural contribution to the production of knowledge*. PhD thesis. Wageningen University. The Netherlands. Available at: www.library.wur.nl/WebQuery/clc/1827406.

Presser, L. (2009) 'The Narratives of offenders', *Theoretical Criminology*, 13.2: 177–200.

Presser, L. (2012) 'Getting on top through mass murder: Narrative, metaphor, and violence' *Crime Media Culture*, 8.1: 3–21.

Richardson, L. and St. Pierre, E. (2005) 'Writing: a method of inquiry', in Denzin, N.K. (ed.) *Handbook of Qualitative Research* (3rd edn), London: Sage.

Said, E. (1978) *Orientalism: Western conceptions of the orient*. London: Penguin.

Simpson, G. and Lewis, P. (2005) 'An investigation of silence and a scrutiny of transparency: Re-examining gender in organization literature through the concepts of voice and visibility', *Human Relations*, 58.10: 1253–1275.

Soin, K. and Scheytt, T. (2006) 'Making the Case for Narrative Methods in Cross-Cultural Organizational Research', *Organizational Research Methods*, 9.1: 55-77.

Sole, D. and Wilson, D.G. (2002) *Storytelling in Organizations: The power and traps of using stories to share knowledge in organizations*, LILA Harvard University, available at: www.providersedge.com/docs/km_articles/Storytelling_in_Organizations.pdf. (Accessed: 27 August 2013).

Strauss, G. (1993) 'The Waiting Wolf', in Zipes, J. (ed.) *Little Red Riding Hood*. 2nd edn. New York: Routledge.

Telegraaf (2012) *Politietop onderschatte project X Haren*. Available at: www.telegraaf.nl/binnenland/21019347/__Project_X_werd_onderschat__.html. (Accessed: 25 March 2013).

Watson, C. (2011) 'Staking a small claim for fictional narratives in social and educational research', *Qualitative Research*, 11.4: 395-408.

Watson, T.J. (2009) 'Narrative, life story and manager identity: A case study in autobiographical identity work', *Human Relations*, 62.3: 425–452.

Weick, K.E. (1995) *Sensemaking in organizations*. Thousand Oaks, CA: Sage.

Youngs, D. and Canter, D.V. (2013) 'Offenders' Crime Narratives as Revealed by the Narrative Roles Questionnaire', *International Journal of Offender Therapy and Comparative Criminology*, 57.3: 289-311.

Youtube (2009) *Australian Savage gang attack Cairns drunk aboriginals abuse cameraman*. Available at: www.youtube.com/watch?v=xGNYeZzXSec. (Accessed: 25 March 2013).

Zipes, J. (ed.) (1993) *Little Red Riding Hood*. 2nd edn. New York: Routledge.

Zipes, J. (1995) *Creative Storytelling: Building Community, Changing Lives*. New York: Routledge.

HAND / HEART / HEAD

Aesthetic Practice Pedagogy for Deep Sustainability Learning*

Vera Ivanaj
University of Lorraine, France

Kim Poldner
University of St Gallen, Switzerland

Paul Shrivastava
Concordia University, Canada

This paper proposes that aesthetic inquiry can convey emotional knowledge related to sustainability topics, which is different from scientific inquiry that conveys facts and analysis. Sustainability is an emotionally charged theme of study and people often have difficulty in grappling with its complexity. We provide a method of art-based learning that can help people to understand and deal with sustainability topics as opposed to classical ways of learning (lectures, coursework). Art is a vehicle of human emotions, and aesthetic inquiry can help to get at the emotional connection between humans and nature. During the 'workshop' process we have developed over the past few years, participants produce paintings, drawings and metaphors that bring life to their vision of sustainability. Expressing this perspective as a work of art and sharing it with others, helps them to better understand underlying concepts, creates a sense of community and gives courage to take action.

- Aesthetic inquiry
- Sustainability
- Aesthetic practices
- Pedagogy
- Art
- Learning

Vera Ivanaj is an Associate Professor of Management Science in the Chemical Engineering School (ENSIC) of the University of Lorraine, France. Her current research interests include strategy, sustainable development, aesthetics, and management education. Vera Ivanaj is also a contemporary painter and works with aesthetic practices and creativity methods to resolve management problems.

✉ ENSIC, University of Lorraine, CEREFIGE, 1, rue Grandville. BP 20451, Nancy, France

💻 vera.ivanaj@univ-lorraine.fr

---

* We are grateful for the useful comments from two anonymous reviewers as well as the editors of the Special Issue, Helen Tregidga and Nick Barter. This work is a fully collaborative effort: the authors have contributed equally.

Kim Poldner is a Research Fellow at the University of St Gallen in Switzerland. Kim's background is in fashion design and organisational theory and her main research interests lie at the interface of sustainability, design/art and entrepreneurship as well as aesthetic and ethnographic methodologies.

University of St. Gallen, Institute for Organizational Psychology, Girtannerstrasse 6, 9010 St. Gallen, Switzerland

kim.poldner@unisg.ch

Paul Shrivastava is the David O'Brien Distinguished Professor and Director of the David O'Brien Centre for Sustainable Enterprise at the John Molson School of Business, Concordia University, Montreal. He leads the International Chair on Arts and Sustainable Enterprise at ICN Business School, France. He has published 15 books and over 100 articles in scholarly and professional journals.

Concordia University and ICN Business School, John Molson School of Business, Concordia University, 1450 Guy Street, Montreal, QC H3G 1M8, Canada

pshrivas@jmsb.concordia.ca

Image 1 Final artwork of the workshop Environmental Crisis realised during the International Conference *Balance Unbalance 2011*, Concordia University, Montreal Canada, 4–5 November 2011

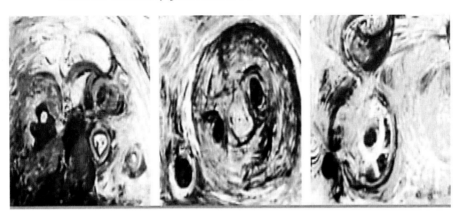

WHAT WOULD YOU DO WITH an empty canvas and a paintbrush to make the world more sustainable? This question was put to managers and scholars with a passion for sustainability. Our goal was to go beyond their academic interest in the topic, and inculcate a holistic understanding and 'living' of complex sustainability challenges. In this paper we propose aesthetic practice pedagogy for sustainability as an integrative approach to learning the values, concepts, community orientation, and courage necessary for moving individuals and organisations towards sustainable practices and policies. Our scholarly aim is to further extend an aesthetical understanding of sustainability organising that can be captured through art-based methods of experiencing and sensing (Shrivastava 2011: 7).

Sustainable development is the greatest challenge facing humanity today (Hart, 2010). Critical ecological, economic and social issues are pressing us to undertake deep changes and transform the human–nature relationship. The climate is changing, the Earth is warming up, biodiversity is declining, current species are facing extinction, hunger and poverty are rampant, energy resources are becoming scarce, pollution is increasing and humans are exceeding the boundaries of what nature can bear (Rockström, 2010). To meaningfully address these problems we need a deep understanding of their real magnitude and interconnections. Our action needs to match the scale of each problem (Xu *et al.*, 2010). We cannot continue to operate and behave as we have been doing, given the rapid deterioration of our global environment. If we want to meet 'the needs of the present generation without compromising the ability of future generations to meet their own needs' (Brundtland Commission, 1987) we need to change individual, societal and organisational behaviours to establish a stable balance between humans and nature.

Education for sustainability

Art, as a testament of human creativity, is a vehicle of human emotions and passion (Shrivastava, Ivanaj, and Ivanaj, 2012). At this time of human, economic and ecological crises, we need creativity and innovation to craft new relationships between humans and nature. We need passionate people who can infuse love and spend energy in the pursuit of sustainability. We have reached the point where cognitive understanding of sustainability is not sufficient to change human behaviour (Chia and Holt, 2008).

> Behaviour change requires among other factors, emotional engagement and passionate commitment. Education for sustainability needs to seriously contend with this basic human fact. Cognitive understanding alone is not sufficient; managers and students need holistic, physical and emotional engagement with sustainability issues (Shrivastava, 2010: 443).

Recent years have seen an increasing interest in how to educate students in business schools to become socially responsible leaders of tomorrow (Wankel and Stoner, 2009; Shrivastava, 2010; Ivanaj and Ivanaj, 2010; Cooperrider and Fry, 2010). Initiatives such as the creation of PRME (United Nations Principles for Responsible Management Education)[1] and 50+20[2] aim to critically examine the role of business, leadership and management education in positively transforming society to resolve social and environmental challenges. Responding to such developments, this journal devoted an entire special issue to the topic of designing management education for a more sustainable future in 2010. Contributions focused on new educational models offering experiential learning (Whiting and de Pillis, 2010; Glunk and Smits, 2010; Broberg and Krull, 2010; Bloom and Pirson, 2010) and specific methods to engage students in deeper, more holistic learning such as meditation and reflection (Schneider, Zollo and Manocha, 2010). The call for proposals for the present special issue together with the encouragement of editors to 'create your own voice', 'be passionate' and 'develop novel, exciting and interdisciplinary approaches to method'[3] in order to develop authentic qualitative research (see for example Bansal and Corley, 2011), has encouraged us to build on these perspectives by articulating the connection between sustainability and art, and describing aesthetic practice learning processes.

Taking into account the role played by art and art-based methods in the education of people (Taylor and Ladkin, 2009; Ryman, Porter and Galbraith, 2009), this paper explores the use of aesthetic practice pedagogy in understanding sustainability and sustainable enterprise. We propose that 'aesthetic inquiry'

---

1 www.unprme.org, accessed 24 May 2014.

2 Management education for the world: www.50plus20.org, accessed 24 May 2014.

3 These recommendations were mentioned by the editors of *Organization*, *Organization Science*, *Organization Studies* and the *Journal of Change Management* during the panel discussion at the EGOS Conference on 5 July 2012.

contributes to conveying emotional and embodied knowledge, which is different from 'scientific inquiry' that conveys facts and analysis. Our desire here is not to juxtapose art and science but to integrate them into a trans-disciplinary approach that can provide a more holistic understanding of sustainability.

Outline of the paper

This paper first explains our understanding of aesthetic inquiry as an integrative form of communication. We then introduce the workshop methodology we have developed and describe and analyse four cases of how it has worked in learning environments. Our experiences suggest that this methodology can help to tackle complexity and specifically the conflicting interpretations and explanations of sustainability. In the conclusion we argue for aesthetic practice pedagogy as a new approach to deep learning about sustainability.

Aesthetic inquiry

Most researchers in the field of organisations and business education take a formal rational approach to 'knowing'. Rational knowledge is the domain of 'science', which is now divided into over 8,000 disciplines, pursuing standardised methods of inquiry, learning and teaching approved within disciplinary communities. This highly cognitive mode of inquiry has been useful in developing 'objective' understanding of the business world and learning about it. But it is not the only form of knowing available to address organisational issues (Chia and Holt, 2008; Bennis and O'Toole, 2005; Ghoshal, 2005). By focusing exclusively on cognitive skills that emphasise abstract concepts, narratives, deductive analysis and technical methods, they ignore the role played by the body and the spirit in the learning process (Shrivastava, 2010: 446). With the traditional approach learners lose their desire to learn. They become distant, detached and dispassionate (Chia and Holt, 2008). At the same time, they are ill-equipped to face the changes of the real world by being 'number crunchers' and analysts rather than managers and leaders (Mintzberg, 2004). In response to these limits there is a call for the creation of alternative forms of knowledge in order to render education more relevant to practice and action. One source of these new forms of knowledge is arts and aesthetics (Taylor and Ladkin, 2009; Ryman, Porter and Galbraith, 2009; Strati, 2007; Adler, 2006).

The aesthetic turn in organisational studies has 'highlighted shortcomings of causal theories of organising' (Strati, 2000: 13) and focuses on corporeality (Linstead and Höpfl, 2000), sensory experience (Taylor and Hansen 2005: 1212), emotional engagement (Shrivastava, 2010), and 'the beautiful' (Adler, 2006;

Strati, 1992). According to Strati (2000: 14), aesthetics can be defined as 'knowing on the basis of sensuous perceptions'. Aesthetics represents a form of emotional knowledge. Experiences within aesthetic processes permit emotional reasoning that creates new senses of reality. The logic behind these experiences includes 'an ability to creatively imagine a future different from the habituated present' (Harter et al., 2008: 426). Thus, 'understanding' through aesthetic rationality is formed jointly on objective reality (Murdoch, 1980), and also on subjective, emotion-based perceptions of reality (Postrel, 2003). Experience in the context of an aesthetical process '…is knowledge producing insofar as it offers a heightened sense of reality pregnant with possibilities, a greater depth of insight…' (Harter et al., 2008: 426). Such experiences engage a progressive inquiry from the spectator who tries to understand and to feel the aesthetically objectivised emotion. The more the spontaneous inquiry goes on, the more she or he feels the inner rhythm, harmony, symbolism and style of the art production. Aesthetics can open our eyes to the beauty beyond our brains and arouse our imagination and emotions, a skill that often seems to be forgotten by adults. As Bengt Johannisson put it: 'Children can intuitively, easily turn imagination into real social projects or artifacts. They have an ability to impulsively affirm and enact upon situated experiences, a natural skill that adults have often learnt to suppress' (Johannisson, 2007: 12).

Aside from imagination, creativity is another key element of aesthetic inquiry. While there are many definitions of creativity as an individual skill, our understanding of this construct is primarily social-relational: it is the result of human interaction and collaboration (Purser and Montuori, 2000). (Inter) actions, occurrences, endeavours are the catalysts for an ongoing becoming or bringing into being of creation. Through trying out, through opening our eyes and hearts and playfully following our intuition, we make creative connections that can shed new light on sustainability (studies). Such a critical, affirmative perspective challenges us to ask different ethical and aesthetical questions (Weiskopf and Steyaert, 2009: 201) with regard to the many facets of sustainability.

An aesthetic approach to studying organisations can draw our attention to forms of knowledge creation that are tacit and sensorial, rather than *a posteriori* constructed (Strati 2000: 13). Organisational aesthetics takes seriously the idea that management is as much an art as it is a science, and applies art-based scholarship and practice to management and organisations. The aesthetical process can lead to 'new cognitive possibilities and a sensibility that is critical of the divisions exercised by modern thought' (Cazeaux, 2000: xiii). In other words, experiences linked to aesthetics can prompt cognitive and emotional reactions. Art is able to qualitatively open different space–time relations from common, ordinary objects. Within the sustainability discourse, the literature has mainly focused on a cognitive understanding of external spaces—such as land, air, water, people—and not on the internal spaces of the human mind and emotions (Shrivastava 2011: 1-2). Caring for the natural environment must first be subjectively experienced, before using objective scientific approaches to understand it. This caring is a cognitively and emotionally driven process, which we will discuss in this article.

Methodology

In this section, we will explain the aesthetic practice pedagogy approach, followed by the workshop format we have developed that has enabled us to 'test' the approach. We conclude this section with a short description of the process of data creation and analysis.

Aesthetic practice pedagogy

Our study takes an 'aesthetic practice' approach to engage organisational members in learning about sustainability concepts and practices by being mentally, emotionally and corporeally involved in the learning process. The methodology we have used is predominantly based on the model of 'aesthetic practice' developed by Debra Orr (2009). Orr (2009: 63) defined aesthetic practice as 'a process in which artistic media are used to engage organisational members in collaborative learning, sense making and change'. Aesthetic practice is an organisational intervention that can be used to develop the ability of people to visualise multiple influences acting on the organisation to develop a vision or a strategy for the future. The visualisation is made possible by using several learning methodologies from the arts.

The theoretical foundations of aesthetic practice method are built on well-established theoretical streams, which are combined to create synergy effects: 'artistic integration, collective co-creation, the expansive qualities of metaphor, and experiential learning' (Orr, 2009: 71-72). Artistic integration refers to the idea that 'truth, emotions, beauty, and values are emergent through art' (Orr, 2009: 71-72). Expansive qualities of metaphor consider that 'learning is accomplished through analogical alignment of a previously known concept with a new concept' (Orr, 2009: 71-72). Collective co-creation posits that 'futures within organisational environments must be co-authored in order to be supported and implemented' (Orr, 2009: 71-72). Experiential learning takes into account the fact that 'people who are actively engaged in a concrete process tend to learn, retain and apply information in ways that may improve their conceptual understanding' (Orr, 2009: 71-72). Participants gain an embodied understanding of sustainability by thinking, acting and feeling collectively. They use metaphors to gain deeper knowledge of the phenomenon, through active interaction and engagement processes. Aesthetic practice methodology is designed to help participants relate to the phenomenon in an integrated way. The pedagogy attempts to render accessible the notion posited by Cooperrider (2001: 30) that 'the artful creation of positive imagery on a collective basis may well be the most prolific activity that individuals and organisations can engage in if their aim is to help bring fruition to a positive and humanly significant future'. While art includes a wide range of activities like theatre, music, poetry, song, dance and culture, in our artistic practice pedagogy we use the artistic medium of painting, to help group members to create a vision and develop sustainable strategies for the future in a collective way.

Workshop format

Our aesthetic practice intervention takes place in the form of a four to six hour workshop with 20 to 40 participants divided into smaller groups of five each. Inspired by the work of Orr (2009), we animate the session by following a six-step methodology, engaging participants to work in small and large groups.

Step 1: Define the problem and the desired outcome
Every workshop starts with an oral and visual presentation of the theme and main question under consideration. This can entail a general discussion of the phenomenon of sustainability or a specific issue relevant to the particular group. The presentations are composed of images that represent pieces of art-work (paintings and drawings) created by one of the researchers, who is also a visual artist.[4] All images are carefully chosen as illustrations of the concept central to each workshop. This selection process is subjective, based on our understanding of the theme, and is meant to create a stimulating atmosphere that will facilitate the creation process. The goal is to, collectively, better under-stand the situation and work on the desired outcomes formulated like a new mission statement.

Step 2: Conceive and paint a metaphor
The next step is that we ask the participants to work in groups of four to five people on developing a metaphor that explains the specific sustainability issue they are tackling. While conceiving this metaphor they are encouraged to brain-storm about desired solutions and the outcomes that they envisage. Then, each group is asked to paint their metaphor by using a variety of art supplies such as different pieces of paper, coloured markers, acrylic colours, pastels, crayons, glitter pens, scissors, glue etc. Taking up these kinds of 'tools' helps participants to engage their mind in a different way from the traditional, rational problem solving.

Step 3: Presentation of metaphors and feedback loop
When the creative expressions of the metaphors are materialised on paper, we invite the participants to give and receive feedback. Paintings are passed from

---

4 Vera Ivanaj, www.pika7.com, accessed 24 May 2014.

one table to another, and each group interprets and explicates the painting of another group, to fully appreciate their meaning. Then the comments are recorded and presented in a plenary session in order to help groups refine and complete their vision.

Step 4: Refine, extend and 'apply the metaphor to reality'

Going back to their small groups, participants extend and refine their metaphors through for example adding details to their painting. Then each group applies the metaphor to 'reality' by formulating future actions to be undertaken in order to resolve the problem.

Step 5: Discussion of future actions

Back in the large group, each smaller group presents their actions and discusses what these actions mean for change. This brainstorm engages everyone to translate their feelings, motivations and creative expressions into acts of change making.

Step 6: Realise a full group painting

The last step is that participants engage in painting one giant common artwork: a painting representing their future vision of the issue at hand. Each participant makes his or her unique contribution while at the same time ensuring a fit with the overall artwork.

Even though every group and every workshop is different, we have experienced that this particular workshop format provides a certain flow that enables the participants to fully engage in the group process of creating a common vision and expressing this vision in a piece of art. The method is currently still being further developed at the International Research Chair for Art and Sustainable Enterprise (IRCASE) in Nancy, France.[5]

Data creation and analysis

So far, we have realised four workshops in different settings. For each session, we collected data using a combination of qualitative methods summarised in Table 1.

During the process we took notes and engaged in participant observation and discussions within and between the groups of participants. We also kept a record of the oral feedback that the different small groups provided to each other. After the artworks had been created, we took photos and made videos of the paintings and drawings. After each session we received a lot of direct feedback from the participants through an evaluation round based on the question 'what

---

5 www.ircase.org, accessed 24 May 2014.

did you experience during this workshop?' In addition we asked participants to provide written feedback within two weeks after the session based on several open questions (see Table 2).

Table 1 Summary of aesthetic practice sessions and data collection processes

Workshops	Main question	Participants	Data collection	Data documentation
1. *Environmental Crisis* November 2011	What can we do— personally and professionally— to improve the situation?	40 people: artists, scientists, economists, philosophers, politicians, sociologists, engineers, management and policy experts	Participant observation & discussion. Participants' oral feed-backs. Analysis of the art works created by the participants.	Researchers' notes. Digital photographs. Video recordings.
2. *Cooperation* September 2011 & September 2012	What can we do to better cooperate?	62 people: Engineering students		
3. *Team spirit* May 2012, October 2012	What can we do to improve team spirit?	69 people: nurses, physiotherapists, dieticians, occupational therapists		
4. *Entrepreneurship* March 2013	What is the added value of your business activity?	20 people: graduate students (engineering, social sciences, management etc.)	Participant observation & discussion. Participants' oral feed-backs. Analysis of the art works created by the participants. Written open-ended questionnaire.	Researcher's notes. Digital photographs. Video recordings. Handwritten responses from the participants.

Table 2 Oral and written open-ended evaluation questions

1.	How did the aesthetic practice workshop engage you in the learning process about your project? a) Mentally, b) Emotionally, c) Corporeally
2.	How did the metaphor influence the understanding and the vision of your project?
3.	How did the act of drawing and painting influence your ideas about the topic of the workshop?
4.	How did the interpretation of drawings and paintings from other groups influence your work?
5.	How did the process of the workshop (working with others, in a structured way, embedded discussions) affect: a) Your own identity b) Your values c) Your relationship to others d) Your view of the project?
6.	What are the learning outcomes of such an experience: a) About you b) About the others c) About your project
7.	How is this experience different from other learning experiences that you have encountered during your training process?
8.	Any other comments to add about this experience?

The entire data creation process resulted in a mixture of textual, visual and auditory material that we inductively analysed. Each author went back and forth between reading, looking at and making sense of the data through highlighting key words and phrases. We then compared these codes, discussed them and filtered the main themes that emerged, which we will discuss in the findings section.

Four cases

Our aesthetic intervention workshops have focused on various sustainability topics and have taken place in different organisations with (academic and professional) participants coming from a range of fields such as engineering, economics, politics, art, management and healthcare. Every workshop started with the presentation of the objectives, the main concepts under consideration and the methodology of aesthetic practice. Then participants engaged mentally, emotionally and manually in the process of creation, following the main steps of our method as presented above. The participants were always volunteers and the workshops were animated by one or two members of our research team. The workshop format was constantly tweaked to make it suitable for the specific group and the examined topic. We need to mention that while the workshops we focus on in this paper have used painting as an art practice, we have also experimented with other art forms (such as music, dance, poetry) as well as sports (running, bicycling, golf, triathlons) as the base for aesthetic pedagogy.

Workshop Environmental Crisis

The first example we like to highlight is the workshop we organised during the international *Balance–Unbalance* conference in Montreal (November 2011).[6] This conference used art as a catalyst to explore intersections between nature, art, science, technology and society. The objective was to reflect, debate and promote projects and actions regarding the environment and human responsibility. Our workshop focused on the ecological aspect of sustainability and had the title 'Aesthetic Practice on Environmental Crisis' (Ivanaj and Shrivastava, 2011). The question we asked was 'What can we do—personally and professionally—to improve the global environmental crisis?' The session brought together 40 conference participants (artists, scientists, economists, philosophers, politicians, sociologists, engineers, management and policy experts) with the intent of engendering a deeper awareness and creating lasting intellectual working partnerships in solving our global environmental crisis. The final artwork realised by the participants was exhibited in the main conference hall (see Image 1).

Workshop Team Spirit

Concerning the social part of sustainability, we have conducted a series of aesthetic practice workshops to build team spirit and motivate people to collaborate effectively. We organised workshops with participants of an executive programme in healthcare management and administration.[7] A first session with 34 people took place in May 2012 and a second session in October 2012, with 35 people. The participants were professionals from different domains (nurses, physiotherapists, dieticians, occupational therapists, etc.) who were all enrolled in a one year educational programme focusing on integrating 'middle' and 'top management' positions in different healthcare public and private organisations in France. During the workshops we focused on the concept of 'team' and the question we asked was 'What can we do to improve the team spirit?' Images 2 and 3 show participants and their artworks.

---

6 www.balance-unbalance2011.hexagram.ca, accessed 24 May 2014.
7 'IFCS' (Institut de Formation des Cadres de la Santé), Nancy, France: www.eicn.chu-nancy .fr/ifcs, accessed 24 May 2014.

Image 2 Artwork produced by the participants of the workshop Team Spirit

Image 3 Participants of the workshop Team Spirit and their artworks

Workshop Cooperation

Related to the social aspect of sustainability, we also conducted workshops with two different groups of engineering students at the engineering school in Nancy.[8] Teachers in the school had complained that it was very difficult to make students work together in teams, which is why the director asked us to undertake workshops with them on the topic of cooperation. The goal was to enhance team spirit and spur success of the students in the programme. The first workshop took place in September 2011 with 28 students and the second one in September 2012 with 34 students. The question we asked was 'What can we do to better cooperate?' Two examples of the artwork realised collectively by these groups are presented in Images 4 and 5.

Image 4 Final artwork of the workshop Cooperation

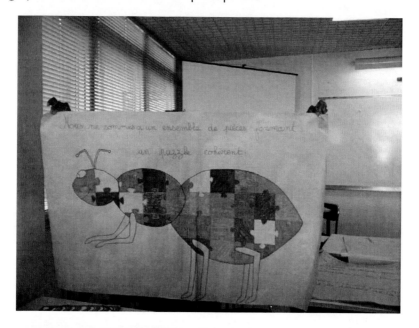

Image 5 Final artwork of the workshop Cooperation

8 Ecole Nationale Supérieure des Industries Chimiques de Nancy (ENSIC), www.ensic.univ-lorraine.fr, accessed 24 May 2014.

Workshop Entrepreneurship

In March 2013 we conducted a session with 20 graduate students of the University of Lorraine around economic aspects of sustainability. The students were all participants of the business incubator of the university[9] and were from a variety of backgrounds such as engineering, social sciences and management. During the time that they were part of this incubator, they received financial as well as educational support and coaching that helped them build their entrepreneurial projects. Our workshop focused on the concept of 'added value' of a new entrepreneurship activity. We asked them the question 'What is the sustainable added value of your business activity?' Examples of their artwork are shown in Image 6.

Image 6 Participants and their final artworks after the workshop
Entrepreneurship

What we scc in Images 1, 2, 4, 5 and 6 is the final artwork co-created by the participants at the end of their session, representing the final vision of the group about the subject under consideration.

---

9 The business incubator is called 'Pole Entrepreneuriat Etudiant de Lorraine' (PEEL), www.le-peel.fr, accessed 24 May 2014.

Findings and discussion

The goal of aesthetic practice pedagogy is to evoke deep personal, emotional understanding and commitment to action. We have observed that the workshops are only the start of the journey to action and a significant part of that voyage is private and subjective. But in the end only the participants are able to recognise the positive results of aesthetic interventions. We summarise these outcomes according to three main points: the learnings, the processes of learning and the change in behaviour and actions. Throughout the analysis, we quote feedback from participants.

What was learned?

One of the main points reported by participants was that aesthetic practice helped them to better understand fundamental aspects of sustainability. Conceiving the problem in a more symbolic form—through drawing, painting and metaphors—provided them with opportunities to create a common frame of reference and better figure out the essential particulars of the problem.

> The metaphor helped us to figure out plenty of other possibilities to work together that we never have thought before. The symbols we used, such as music, animals, etc. allowed us to better understand what was really important for our group. The variety of representations expanded our vision (workshop Cooperation).

Symbols and visual representations in the artworks were often inspired by nature and were usually very evocative. The sun, flowers, trees, leaves, clouds, water, mountains and people are easily recognised based on human sensual experience related to the natural world. The sun represents warmth and energy while trees and leaves can represent for example the biodiversity on our planet. What became obvious is that people were able to see more things in a painting than they could describe in words.

> In the beginning it was difficult to express through metaphors but then we realised how powerful it is to help our understanding of the project (workshop Entrepreneurship).

In this respect Weick suggested (1995: 49) 'a metaphor can often capture some of these distinctive powerful, private realities that are tough to describe to someone else'. Symbols and metaphors help to translate complex sustainability issues into more elementary compositions that help participants to understand and give meaning.

> The metaphor put me in the mood, made me comfortable with the project and really helped me focus (workshop Environmental Crisis).

The cognitive complexity of problems was better revealed through a variety of angles and options integrated into the paintings. As noticed by Booth (1997: 96), symbolism 'is the natural process by which people make bridges between things, between a discernible symbol and something more abstract we want to understand'. As we have argued in an earlier article, 'art has the unique ability to symbolise complex abstractions in concrete ways, which yield the potential for raising awareness and bringing about a shift in mindset, necessary for sustainability' (Shrivastava, Ivanaj and Ivanaj, 2012: 29). As one workshop participant looks back:

> The act of drawing is very close to me, I have been drawing since I can remember from the age of four or five. So, consequently the act of drawing and painting really drew me in to the topic of the workshop and I was totally intrigued by the concept (workshop Environmental Crisis).

Through focusing on one of the artworks, we can better understand the importance of symbolism. Image 4 (workshop Cooperation) is an example of a metaphor and a drawing conceived by a group in the beginning of the creation process, working on the concept of team cooperation. The metaphor conceived by the group to illustrate the concept is written on the top of the image: 'We all are part of one entity, creating a coherent puzzle' ('Nous ne sommes qu'en ensemble de pieces formant un puzzle coherent'). The image shows an ant composed of a multitude of small, colourful parts. The ant is chosen to symbolise the whole team, which has to work hard (like an ant) to succeed. Each small part of the puzzle represents a member of the team that originally is different from the others (different colours). These differences taken separately could be seen as a threat to group cooperation, but at the same time they represent complementary resources. To become a resource each individual has to be connected to the others and to be placed in the right place (like in a puzzle), otherwise the team cannot perform. Some individuals are placed in the head part of the ant. That means that they have to play an important role as team leaders. Some others are placed in the middle part of the ant and they represent connectors. The majority of the individuals are placed in the bottom part of the ant and they symbolise the followers. The ant stands up on its hind legs, and looks like it is searching for a direction. That implied the team's need for setting up clear objectives based on a coherent strategy and vision for the future.

The process of learning was facilitated through a deep involvement based on a positive experience and an act of creating. The embodied practice of putting colours on a canvas rendered the learning process very attractive.

> Using our hands through the painting made us feel that we were deeply in touch with our project. The bodily involvement came naturally to us and we didn't care about the fact that we got dirty (workshop Entrepreneurship).

By creating forms and images, by choosing beautiful colours, by introducing changes and improving the paintings progressively, participants were deeply immersed in a consensual collective collaboration. As noticed by Taylor and Ladkin (2009: 56), the great benefit of art-based methods of learning such as drawing, music, paintings, sculpture, story and drama is that they represent this specific 'presentational' form of knowing that 'provides relative direct access to our felt experience and draws upon our emotional connection to our self, others and our experience. Propositional methods and forms filter out the feeling and emotion in pursuit of precision, clarity, and objectivity'. Through drawing and paintings—through various forms of imagery—participants accessed embodied sensuous knowing, which is different from 'propositional knowing' that concentrates on ideas and theories expressed in information statements (Heron and Reason, 2001: 183). As one workshop participant recalled:

> I learnt a lot about myself, or at the time I thought I did. I really enjoyed the final painting and outcome with the coordinator and person overseeing the project. I remember being very excited about this outcome. It was very wet paint and we had to figure out how to move it to an exhibition venue while it was still wet. I also remember I felt a bit odd because I'd splashed paint over a few of the other participants but I didn't really care. I felt really free and loose with painting and drawing and I'm very grateful for that experience. It was one of the most liberating things I experienced at a particularly stuffy conference I attended in Montreal and I'll always remember it (workshop Environmental Crisis).

The process of learning

A collaborative and supportive process stimulates creativity and a shift in mindset. Through mindful and constructive feedback, original views and ideas were enriched and participants started seeing the problem in different ways.

> We wanted to respect the wishes of everyone and we all contributed in a natural way. We learned to be in peace with ourselves and with others (workshop Cooperation).

By using multiple sense capabilities in a non-judgemental environment, participants felt free and proud of their creation. They realised that they have the ability to create beautiful artwork without the need to be professionally trained artists. After the workshop they often felt happy and more self-confident to continue to express their creativity.

> Drawing and painting helped us to work instinctively. The beginning was difficult but after the first group of people began to draw, we saw what they were able to do: beautiful things. That helped us feel more self-confident (workshop Team Spirit).

The trust and cohesion created in the group, through working and sharing together, helped them to succeed even though in the beginning of the process they had doubts and did not feel confident with the process of aesthetic practice. In fact, the expression of the emotions and sharing creativity in a group created a positive effect, which was very motivating and fun. Taking pleasure in accomplishment helped participants to persist and fix priorities. Positive feelings and enthusiasm encouraged learning and rendered people passionate.

> We (re)discovered the joy of learning, avoiding too much rationality and seriousness, which does not motivate so much (workshop Entrepreneurship).

Passion facilitated courage and mobilised the human energy, which helped to overcome difficulties and encouraged people to change without resistance (Smollan, 2006).

We felt more responsible for our future and we wanted to create our future by ourselves (workshop Cooperation).

This illustrated how passion has real transformational power to move people towards sustainability (Shrivastava, 2010).

The action and behavioural changes

The aesthetic practice sessions brought together people who very often did not know each other. They got to know the members of their group by working on the same drawings and paintings and by sharing values, thoughts, feelings, supplies and space. They also discovered more about their own personalities and competences.

People designed various objects that are dear to them or that characterise them better. We could see what was most important in their lives and why they were interested to collaborate (workshop Cooperation).

Participants told us that they were amazed to see how others proceeded with the paintings they themselves had been working on: how they started working, how they mixed the colours, how they felt about their work.

It was just a very direct, immediate and creative opening to an inner impulse, which I wish I could access all the time! I will never forget it, it brings back the most immediate and focused experience, I would like to do this much more in my creative life (workshop Environmental Crisis).

Participants benefited from the individual experience of others and wanted to support and improve their projects. By working in a collaborative way, by sharing positive emotional energy and by co-creating beautiful artwork, participants built strong and close relationships between each other.

The drawing made us feel unified and being part of a team. We reached consensus very fast and every one made a real contribution (workshop Entrepreneurship).

Through artistic expression, they learned to move in the same direction simultaneously towards the creation of a shared vision. The satisfaction of the desire to be part of the group contributed to building trust and created cohesion between the members of the group.

Implications

Aesthetic practice pedagogy is the application of aesthetic inquiry to teaching, learning and action. In the context of sustainability it involves getting participants to gain a deeply felt understanding of sustainability challenges and to develop the courage necessary to evoke actions. Standard classroom lecture-oriented learning is not able to evoke such deep responses from students and managers. It is effective in conveying information and issues, but often fails to motivate behaviour. For behavioural engagement of students and managers in sustainability practices in and out of organisations we need a more engaging pedagogy that involves connection through a cognitive, bodily and emotional medium that focuses on sustainability.

Our approach to aesthetic practice pedagogy is the development of the 3H-model of hand, heart and head. First, participants use their *hands* (and body) by picking up a paintbrush, canvas, paints and being in the physical space with others, visualising and materialising what sustainability means to them. Second, in a safe and supportive environment encouraged by each other and coaches, their emotions start flowing (*heart*) and they get engaged in an embodied 'knowing'. When emotions are awakened, the brain (*head*) gets a much deeper understanding of the meaning of sustainability. The benefits of this approach are that workshop participants are intensely involved in *doing* something (artistic) together and this experience leads to a holistic understanding of the topic under focus. The process of creating value together brings about strong bonds between the participants and strengthens cycles of learning, understanding and making sense of sustainability. Participants also reported an exceptional sensation of being happy and a feeling of empowerment to shape a better world. Aside from these direct outcomes experienced by the participants, others also reported tangible results. The teachers in the engineering school who had complained about the lack of cooperation skills of their students, reported a great improvement in team work after the workshops. In summary, aesthetic practice pedagogy engages participants in reflection and action on sustainability and can be highly effective in developing:

▶ **Holistic systems thinking**. Recognising patterns and relationships across disparate information and knowledge systems with a focus on holistic understanding and experience

▶ **Systems practice**. Developing imaginative forms, processes, and solutions that communicate or create new relationships and patterns across disciplines

▶ **Emotional experience**. Engages subjects and groups in affective ways arousing deep interests and feeling for the topic under study

▶ **Team building**. Working in cross-disciplinary collaborations, respecting what team members bring to problem solving

▶ **Team process**. Facilitating democratic and just decision making, sharing power and responsibility, and applying conflict resolution when needed

▶ **Project assessment**. Building feedback loops into processes to constructively evaluate individual and team efforts so that methodologies and outcomes can be more effective and resilient

▶ **Improvisation and creativity**. Working in dynamic environments with uncertain resources to conceptualise and execute real time action toward achieving goals

▶ **Creativity/Innovation**. Making new connections and seeing new patterns

▶ **Leadership**. Awareness and sensitivity to making co-workers effective

▶ **Aesthetic values** and **aesthetic rationality**

We recommend further testing of the 3H-model including the use of other art forms, working with different target groups and focusing on a larger variety of sustainability-related topics. In addition we recommend encouraging participants to provide a second round of feedback 6 to 12 months after the workshop has taken place. This longitudinal perspective would reveal how much knowledge and action has been retained.

Conclusion

In this paper we proposed aesthetic practice pedagogy as a way to convey deep emotional learning about sustainability. Science helps to understand some (rational) aspects of sustainability but not other (emotional) aspects. Art is a vehicle of human emotions and aesthetic inquiry is a mode of inquiry to get at that emotional connection between humans and nature needed for sustainability. As such, we perceive that aesthetic practice and art-based methods can be very powerful methods to help people to understand, express, share and implement very complex concepts like 'sustainable strategy', 'sustainable leadership' and 'intergenerational equity' in the context of business.

We have offered several examples of workshops with managers and scholars where we applied aesthetic practice pedagogy to move them beyond (scientific) explanation of sustainability and onto art-inspired action. During the workshop process, participants produced paintings, drawings and metaphors in small groups that brought to life a vision or a strategy related to sustainability. Expressing such a strategy/vision as a work of art instead of as a written report helped them to better understand the concept and gain confidence to act on their knowledge. Furthermore, when these artworks are shared in the larger group, it brings a sense of consensus and commonality between the participants and this prepares them optimally for taking action. Our findings thus far show that art-based methods can really make a difference for participants to understand and deal with sustainability topics as opposed to the classical way of learning (lectures, coursework). Aesthetic practice pedagogy can build a bridge between embodying, feeling and knowing about sustainability: between hand, heart and head. We envisage that this 3H-model can assist scholars, managers, entrepreneurs and students to really engage in sustainability on a deeper intuitive and emotional level while generating a strong feeling of positive connectedness to each other and a better future. We will thus continue to develop this method with the aim to inspire more people to deeply engage with sustainability issues.

References

Adler, N. J. (2006) 'The Arts and Leadership: Now That We Can Do Anything, What Will We Do?' *Academy of Management Learning and Education* 5.4: 486-499.

Bansal, P. and Corley, K. (2011) 'From the Editors. The Coming of Age for Qualitative Research: Embracing the Diversity of Qualitative Methods', *Academy of Management Journal* 54.2: 233-237.

Bennis, W. and J.O. O'Toole (2005) 'How Business Schools Lost Their Way', *Harvard Business Review* 83.5: 98-104.

Bloom, G. and Pirson, M. (2010) 'Supporting Social Change Agents through the Classroom: The SE Lab Model (Unleashing a Rising Generation of Leading Social Entrepreneurs: An Emerging University Pedagogy)', *Journal of Corporate Citizenship 39:* 103-111.

Booth, E. (1997) *The Everyday Work of Art: How Artistic Experience Can Transform Your Life,* Naperville, IL: Sourcebooks.

Broberg, T. and Krull, P. (2010) 'Where Creativity and Innovation Go to School: A Case Study of the KaosPilot School of Leadership and Social Entrepreneurship', *Journal of Corporate Citizenship 39:* 57-86.

Brundtland Commission (1987) *Our Common Future,* United Nations World Commission on Environment and Development, Oxford University Press: Oxford, New York.

Cazeaux, C. (2000) *The Continental Aesthetics Reader,* London: Routledge.

Chia, R. and R. Holt (2008) 'The Nature of Knowledge in Business Schools', *Academy of Management Learning and Education* 7.4: 471-486.

Cooperrider, D. (2001) 'Positive Image, Positive Action: The Affirmative Basis for Organizing', In Cooperrider, Sorenson, Yaeger and Whitney (eds.). *Appreciative Inquiry: An Emerging Direction for Organizational Development.* Champaign, IL: Stipes Publishing, LLC.

Cooperrider, D. and Fry, R. (2010) 'Editorial. Developing Tomorrow's Business Leaders to Enact Corporate Citizenship: The Call and Opportunity for B-Schools to Make an Enduring Difference', *Journal of Corporate Citizenship 39:* 3-5.

Ghoshal, S. (2005) 'Bad Management Theories are Destroying Good Management Practices', *Academy of Management Learning and Educa*tion 4.1: 75-91.

Glunk, U. and Smits, M. (2010) 'Turning Point: Awakening World-Changing Leadership through Management Education', *Journal of Corporate Citizenship 39:* 87-91.

Hart, S. (2010) *Capitalism at the Crossroads: Next-Generation Business Strategies for a Post-Crisis World,* 3rd edn, Wharton School Publishing: Upper Saddle River, NJ.

Harter, L.M., Leeman, M., Norander, S., Young, S.L, & Rawlins, W.K. (2008) 'The Intermingling of Aesthetic Sensibilities and Instrumental Rationalities in a Collaborative Arts Studio', *Management Communication Quarterly,* 21: 423-453.

Heron, J. and Reason, P. (2001) 'The Practice of Co-operative Inquiry: Research "with" Rather than "on" People'. In P. Reason & H. Bradbury (Eds.), *Handbook of Action Research: Participative Inquiry and Practice:* 179-188, London: Sage.

Hjorth, D. and Steyaert, C. (2009) *The Politics and Aesthetics of Entrepreneurship,* Cheltenham: Edward Elgar.

Ivanaj, V. and Ivanaj, S. (2010) 'The Contribution of Interdisciplinary Skills to Sustainability of Business: When Artists, Engineers, and Managers work together to serve Enterprises', In Stoner, J.A.F. and Wankel, C. (Eds.): *Global Sustainability as a Business Imperative*, pp. 91–109, Palgrave Macmillan.

Ivanaj, V. and Shrivastava, P. (2011) Workshop on 'Aesthetic Practice on Environmental Crisis, International Conference', at the *Balance–Unbalance 2011 Conference*, Concordia University, Montreal Canada, 4–5 November, www.balance-unbalance2011.hexagram.ca.

Johannisson, B. (2007) '(Be)fore Words'. In D. Hjorth and M. Kostera (Eds.), *Entrepreneurship and the Experience Economy*, (pp. 11-16), Copenhagen: Copenhagen Business School Press.

Linstead, S. and Höpfl, H. (2000) *The Aesthetics of Organization*, London: Sage.

Mintzberg, H. (2004) *Managers not MBAs*, London, New York: Prentice Hall.

Murdoch, I. (1980). *The Sovereignty of Good*, Cambridge: Cambridge University Press.

Orr, D. (2009) 'Aesthetic Practice: The Power of Artistic Expression to Transform Organizations', *Revue Sciences de Gestion*, 70: 63-82.

Postrel, V. (2003) *The Substance of Style: How the Rise of Aesthetic Value Is Remaking Commerce, Culture, and Consciousness*, New York: HarperCollins Publishers.

Purser, R.E. and Montuori, A. (2000) 'In Search of Creativity: Beyond Individualism and Collectivism'. Paper presented at the *Western Academy of Management Conference*, 8 April 2000 Kona, Hawaii.

Rockström, J. (2010) 'Planetary Boundaries', *New Perspectives Quarterly*, Vol. 27, No. 1, pp. 72–74.

Ryman, J., Porter, T., and Galbraith, C. (2009) 'Disciplined Imagination: Art and Metaphor in the Business School Classroom', *International Journal of Education & the Arts*, 10(10) (www.ijea.org/v10n10, accessed 18 September 2013).

Schneider, S., Zollo, M. and Manocha, R. (2010) 'Developing Socially Responsible Behaviour in Managers: Experimental Evidence of the Effectiveness of Different Approaches to Management Education', *Journal of Corporate Citizenship 39*: 21-40.

Shrivastava, P. (2010) 'Pedagogy of Passion for Sustainability', *Academy of Management Learning and Education 9.3*: 443–455.

Shrivastava, P. (2011) 'Enterprise Sustainability 2.0: Aesthetics of Sustainability', In A. Hoffman and T. Bansal (Eds.), *The Oxford Handbook of Business and the Natural Environment*. Pratim: Oxford University Press.

Shrivastava, P., Ivanaj, V. and Ivanaj, S. (2012) 'Sustainable Development and the Arts', *International Journal of Technology Management 60*, 1/2: 23–43.

Smollan, R.K. (2006) 'Minds, Hearts and Deeds: Cognitive, Affective and Behavioural Responses to Change', *Journal of Change Management 6*. 2: 143-158.

Strati, A. (1992) 'Aesthetic Understanding of Organizational Life', *Academy of Management Review 17.3*: 568-581.

Strati, A. (2000) *Organization and Aesthetics*, London: Sage.

Strati, A. (2007) 'Sensible Knowledge and Practice-based Learning', *Management Learning*, 38.1: 61-77.

Taylor, S. and Hanson, H. (2005) 'Finding Form: Looking at the Field of Organizational Aesthetics', *Journal of Management Studies 42.6*: 1211-32.

Taylor, S.S. and D. Ladkin (2009) 'Understanding Art-based Methods in Managerial Development, *Academy of Management Learning and Education 8.1*: 55-69.

Wankel, C., and J. A. F. Stoner. (2009) *Management Education for Global Sustainability*, Charlotte, NC: Information Age Publishing, Inc.

Weggeman, M. and Lammers, I. (2007) 'Aesthetics from a Design Perspective', *Journal of Organizational Change Management 20.3*: 346-358.

Weick, K. (1995) Sensemaking in Organizations, Thousand Oaks, CA: Sage.

Weiskopf, R. and Steyaert, C. (2009) 'Metamorphoses in Entrepreneurship Studies: Towards an Affirmative Politics of Entrepreneuring' In D. Hjorth and C. Steyaert (Eds.), *The Politics and Aesthetics of Entrepreneurship* (pp. 183-201). Cheltenham: Edward Elgar.

Whiting, V. and de Pillis, E. (2010) 'A Five-Phase Approach to Poverty Eradication: An Educational Proposal for Sustainable Leadership and Sustainable Development', *Journal of Corporate Citizenship 39*: 41-56.

Xu, M., Crittenden, J.C., Chen, Y., Thomas, V.M., Noonan, D.S., Brown, M.A. and French, S.P. (2010) 'Gigaton Problems need Gigaton Solutions', *Environmental Science & Technology 44*.1: 4037–4041.

Is this OK?

An Exploration of Extremes

Nick Barter and Luke Houghton

Griffith University, Australia

This paper presents an abridged version of a fictional story titled 'Is this OK?', a story about a day in the life of an individual in a non-specific future. It was written as a teaching aid to help students critically engage with theory, as experience has taught the authors that students' engagement with conventional academic articles is problematic. There are three principal theories that inform the story, notwithstanding that the piece also alludes to other contemporary issues and a reader is likely to identify the influence of a variety of theoretical constructs. The three are natural capital, companies selling solutions rather products or services and a construct of humans as being a temporal negotiation between their genetic material and the environment they find themselves in. The first two concepts are, as the article discusses, encapsulated within but not limited to the concept of natural capitalism. The third draws on a construct of a human as being a phenotype. It should be noted that while the story can be read as polemic, this is not the intent, rather the intent is to invoke questioning and reflection to aid critical development.

● Natural capital
● Human being
● Fiction
● Metaphor

Nick Barter is a senior lecturer in strategy and sustainability and is the MBA director at Griffith. Prior to Griffith he spent 5 years at the University of St Andrews in the UK. His current research includes metaphors and conceptions of the environment.

✉ Griffith Business School, Griffith University, Room 4.26, Building S07, Southbank Campus, PO Box 3370, South Brisbane, QLD 4101, Australia

▢ n.barter@griffith.edu.au

Luke Houghton is a senior lecturer in management and information systems at the Griffith Business School where he has worked since 2004. His research is focused on engagement strategies for wicked problems, the impact of large systems on work processes and blended learning strategies in higher education.

✉ Griffith Business School, Griffith University, Room 1.2.1 Macrossan Building, Nathan Campus, Nathan QLD 4111, Australia

▢ l.houghton@griffith.edu.au

THIS ARTICLE PRESENTS AN ABRIDGED version of 'Is this OK?', a story about an individual's day in a non-specific future. The story was written as a teaching aid to help higher education students explore the impact of theory when refracted through an extreme. The paper begins by discussing the context surrounding the writing of the story, explaining the anecdotal observations that prompted the piece, the key theories that informed the authors when writing and the process of completing the original publication. Following the context an abridged version of the story is presented, and the key themes brought forward in the abridged version are discussed. The paper finishes with an endnote on metaphors and the terminology of 'natural capital' and by extension 'natural capitalism'.

Context

The writing of 'Is this OK?' was inspired by two key factors. The first was higher education students' lack of engagement with academic material. The second, the authors' concerns regarding students' lack of critical engagement and thus their non-consideration of the implications of theories, particularly if those theories are applied to an extreme; with the extreme being a refractive device to enable learning. It has been argued that a key part of higher education is that it is a transformative learning experience (Mezirow, 1994) where key to that experience is students' developing the ability to critique. However an issue with developing these skills is ensuring students read academic articles in the first place. Anecdotally at least, many university lecturers would join a chorus of how students do not read academic articles. Thus developing students' critical skills is difficult if in the first instance they do not actually read the articles. This lack of reading of academic articles is perhaps to be expected, especially as a standard academic article is not necessarily written in plain English and to quote one student known to the authors, a standard article is presented to the reader as an impenetrable 'wall of text'. Given this situation, the authors decided to develop a fictional story, which would be informed by theories, with the hope that this would be more readily acceptable to students. The basic premise being that if the theory or theories are encapsulated within a fictional story they are more accessible to the student reader; this accessibility in turn enables the student reader to develop critical skills that might otherwise be avoided because of the impenetrability of a standard academic article.

The three key theories that informed the writing of the piece were: 1) the concept of natural capital; 2) companies selling solutions rather products or services; and 3) a construct of humans as being a temporal negotiation between their genetic material and the environment they find themselves in. The first two are encapsulated within but not limited to the concept of natural capitalism (Hawken *et al.*, 1999). The third concerns humans being phenotypes that are in a state of constant negotiation between their genotypes and the environment (Ingold, 2011).

Explaining further how each of these theories informed the piece, natural capitalism argues that it is an approach that represents 'what capitalism might become if its largest category of capital—the natural capital of ecosystem services—were properly valued' (Hawken *et al.*, 1999:146). The theory has within it four key tenets: to dramatically increase the productivity of natural resources; shift to biologically inspired production models; move to a solutions based model; and reinvest in natural capital. The first two of these tenets are not overtly explored within the story, while the last two are. With regard to moving to a solutions-based model, this is the notion that companies should consider the underlying need that is being solved by their product or service. For example, rather than sell cars, companies should explore selling transport services and perhaps rather than sell light bulbs a company might want to explore selling illumination services. This concept of considering the underlying need or problem that is being solved is similar to that propagated by Levitt (1960) in his seminal article 'Marketing Myopia'. Levitt (1960) argued, for example, that the rail companies should see themselves in the transport business and oil companies in the energy business. The concept of a solutions-based model weaves its way into 'Is this OK?' through descriptions of, for example, the shaving company being in the business of keeping the protagonist free from facial hair as opposed to it being in the business of selling razors. As such the shaving company offers advice on how to maximise the time of being clean shaven and charges for each shave rather than selling a razor.

Inherent to the concept of *Natural Capitalism* (Hawken *et al.*, 1999) is the notion that natural capital is properly valued. Natural capital is not specifically defined by Hawken *et al.* (1999) beyond alluding to it being equivalent to ecosystem services. Elsewhere Porritt (2006) defines natural capital as 'that part of the natural world which we humans make some use of or derive some benefit from' (Porritt, 2006: 123). Parts of the natural world and/or an ecosystem service that we derive some benefit from are, for example, the oxygen we breathe or the aesthetic beauty and sense of well-being an individual derives from being in a place of wildlife and trees (Porritt, 2006). In an extreme the value of natural capital may be monetary. This extreme is explored within the story of 'Is this OK?' by the protagonist paying for the oxygen he breathes. Similarly he pays to be able to sit next to a tree on his coffee break as it offers an aesthetic value and a sense of well-being.

Building upon the concept of paying for ecosystem services and natural capital being valued, a further influence on the writing of 'Is this OK?' was the 1997 paper by Costanza *et al.* This paper valued the world's ecosystem services (excluding the oceans) at $33 trillion compared to a global gross domestic product, at that time, of $18 trillion. When viewed purely through dollar terms, the calculations by Costanza *et al.* (1997) indicate that the monetisation of ecosystem services is a potential growth opportunity for industries, a potential revenue stream of $33 trillion. The story of 'Is this OK?' takes the notion of valuing ecosystem services and conveys, through fiction, some of the potential implications of putting a monetary value to the exchanges people have with natural capital, for example, breathing and sitting next to a tree.

The third principal theory that informed the story of 'Is this OK?' was a model of humans as being phenotypes that are in a state of constant negotiation between their genotypes and the environment (Ingold, 2011). This concept argues that what makes a human human is not purely genetics, but rather a human is a negotiation of intrinsic and extrinsic attributes—a nexus of the relationship between genetics and environment. This construct indicates that humans need to be considered as an expression of a particular field of relationships between genetics and environment where they are not separable from either. This in turn drives at the core of what it means to be a human, as being human is no longer purely defined by genetic code, rather a human is a temporal mix of genetic code and relationships, none of which are separable (Ingold, 2001, 2011). The implication of this is that our understanding of what it might mean to be a human is temporal. This temporality pervades the story whereby the protagonist continually accepts the situations he finds himself in, for example the constant real time monitoring of his work performance relative to other workers across the globe. The temporal understanding is also where the story of 'Is this OK?' ends. At the end the protagonist is very accepting of the current naming convention applied to humanity relative to that of the past. He finds that the definition of a human being has changed, yet he is at ease with this realisation as the definition fits with and makes sense to him within his future world.

The temporal understanding of humanity, offering services not products and the valuing of ecosystem services are the key theories that informed the writing of the story and were, as best could be, applied to an extreme. In presenting them through fiction it is hoped that readers can reflect on present day theories and in so doing develop critical faculty to consider the potential impacts of such theories. As although theories may fit with a moment in time, 'Is this OK?' attempts to highlight how the application of current day theories could have potentially challenging (relative to current day) future implications.

Finally prior to presenting the abridged version of 'Is this OK?', it is worthwhile discussing some of the practical aspects of writing and publishing the story. The story was written via an email exchange, where one author would write a paragraph and then the other would add to it and continue the story and then send it back. After reaching a point of conclusion, the story was edited down from c. 7,000 words to c. 4,000 words. The complete, non-abridged version of the story was embellished by the addition of imagery inspired by the text. Weiler (2004) has argued that conventionally the use of imagery has been viewed as time wasting. However in the modern, image-saturated world imagery may be a necessary component in order to encourage reader engagement (Weiler, 2004; Hoover, 2012). Given this and based on the authors' own views, imagery was added. The complete version of 'Is this OK?' was self-published in January 2013. The complete version has supporting notes to aid the facilitator who may use the story as a teaching aid. It can be downloaded for no charge at www .isthisokay.com.

Is This OK? Abridged version

He awoke a little foggy headed. It had not been a bad night's sleep but something was troubling him and he wasn't sure what. He looked across at the bedside table through the slits created by his half-open eyes. It was 7.03 a.m., 28 degrees Celsius outside (in the middle of winter) and according to the rolling text along the bottom of the display, Newland, the farthest south a town had ever been built, was in for a scorcher. Unfortunately the bedside display also told him something he didn't want to know, his credit balance and net worth. He had 400 credits in his account and his net worth was less than it was yesterday. He groaned, closed his eyes and rolled over. Then a second later he kicked himself into action with the thought that 400 credits was not much, he needed to get to work and boost his balance. He hadn't been to work for the past few days due to illness and he had watched his balance decrease, a numerical reminder that reinforced the sense of worthlessness that typically came with illness. Particularly because, due to illness, he had used the bathroom more often and as such been charged extra by the utilities company for the increased usage.

He sat up, turned to get out of bed, and felt the call of nature. 'No', he thought, 'I will hold on, I have spent enough with the utility company recently, charging me and even analysing my outputs to recommend doctors, remedies and output reduction strategies. I will use the bathroom at work, I don't pay for it'. He took one more look at the bedside display, it flashed in amber that he had prepaid for oxygen up until Saturday, it was now Thursday. 'Great' he thought 'well at least they don't charge kids. They don't get charged until they are twenty one years old.' He looked at his net worth and decided to use some to pay for a chunk of oxygen. The way his net worth was decreasing he would be worth nothing to society by the time he was 65. 'What the heck', he thought, he pressed the button and his net worth decreased, his projected net worth of zero was now forecast to be 64.5 years.

Finally he got out of bed; he knew it made sense to be on the transporter before 8 a.m. when the peak fares hit. Last year he had slept past his alarm and had to pay the peak fare as well as the peak oxygen levy. He made his way into the bathroom to look at the mirror. His face was unshaven. Could he get away with it? Was he seeing anyone important today? He had thought of growing a beard but the patchy stubble made him look ridiculous. He picked up his shaver and turned on the tap. As he did so he checked the bathroom display. The estimated cost of a shave right now was 3 credits. 'Damn' he thought, it had gone up since yesterday. The display outlined how Shave Co had increased their prices but now their new connected shave blade allowed better, closer shaving and because of that the price had gone up. His mind wandered for a second; real time information, real time prices for shaving, everything monitored, everything a transaction. To encourage him to shave now a follow up message came on the display, telling him if he shaved now he wouldn't have to do it again for 36 hours based on the information they held on him. He ignored this information and continued brushing his teeth; one credit was debited by Teeth Clean Co. As he brushed advice came up on the display about his optimal brushing technique, a new toothpaste and good local dentists. The display was about to switch to the state of his teeth; however rather than this he gestured so that information would shrink away and the news would be displayed. The chief finance minister was on discussing how Newland had kept its credit rating and the credit agency's outlook for Newland was good. Following this the news commentator brought up a graph showing how Newland had maintained its rating for the past five years. 'Now there was something to be proud of' he thought. His mind wandered to when he was a child and he had been a scout and earned stars for good deeds. The symmetry between that and Newland earning a good credit rating seemed appropriate.

After brushing his teeth he went back to the bedroom and got dressed. His wife was sitting up in bed.

'You aren't shaving?' she said.

'I will do it at work. Cheaper,' he said.

He put on his clothes; they weren't fashionable just functional. Functional was all he could afford, the fashionable clothing companies had stopped selling to him, because he didn't fit the image profile they wanted. Something to do with his likes and preferences was the excuse the fashion labels offered. He felt sure it was his credit balance that mattered, he was sure if he had more credit his likes and preferences would be overlooked by the fashion companies. He cast his mind back to the last time he had bought a shirt, the best offer he had was from DIY Co. They had been the only company that had offered him a discount on the shirt price if he agreed to use his chest as an advertising hoarding for them. As he put the shirt on and ran his thumb over the DIY logo he remembered how when buying the shirt a voluptuous young woman was buying a top at the next display. She had been offered a 75% discount on the price if she agreed to use her chest to advertise a fashion company. Of course she had taken the offer. Who wouldn't? A 75% discount is great. She bought the top, took the discount and walked out with a logo emblazoned across her. When he had been buying his top, the DIY store had offered 5%. He wondered what it would be like to be so rich that you didn't display advertising on your clothes. He briefly wandered around that whimsical thought, giggled and remembered how his grandfather had talked about when people used to pay more so they could walk around with a big brand emblazoned on their clothes. He chuckled to himself at how people were so silly in times past; paying more to have brand advertising, not less.

He went through to the kitchen and flicked the kettle on. The electricity meter counted up the increments and reminded him that payment was taken at the end of every day. He stopped the kettle halfway through and made himself a lukewarm coffee. He thought about his lunch break and the opportunity to sit by the tree. The tree in its protective cabinet standing among the buildings; it was a place he went to, to be at peace. It may cost more to sit near the tree but it was worth it, it was his one indulgence and it helped. He ate his cereal, drank his coffee and then walked out the front door.

Outside he put on his Oxygen Co respirator. He did not notice the dense, smoggy air; it was everywhere and always there so there was no reason why he should notice. The intake valve on his respirator rattled and he felt comfortable, he was off to work.

JCC 54 *June 2014*

The display in the respirator flashed a warning message and he heard a clicking sound followed by a muffled voice from the earpiece of his respirator, 'Please note, the current market rate for oxygen via this mask is 1 credit per oxygenated hour'. The display then offered some instructions on how he could maximise the value he could get from his respirator followed by the share price of the Oxygen Co and a buy now indicator. He motioned with his eyes and the display turned off. He walked to the transporter station.

He got off at the transport station near his work, the credits for the fare were automatically taken and it began to rain. He took out the umbrella from his bag. As he put it up, his display brought forward a message from the umbrella company, a smiling cartoon type umbrella began to say how he was using state of the art technology to keep himself dry and that there would be a small charge of 0.25 credits for using it, because Umbrella Co was in the business of 'keeping you dry, not making umbrellas'. As he walked on his display listed another charge being taken by the city municipality for draining the water that was collecting from him from the downpour. He sighed and smiled, it had always been like this and besides he knew there was no alternative.

He continued walking but as he did his mind wandered and he wondered whether life was just a game that submitted to a master dichotomy of consumption and production, spending and earning, a game of keeping in positive credit so consumption could continue. He made it to the tower that housed his workstation; once inside he removed his respirator. He went into the lift and got out on his floor. As he reached his workstation his holocomputer began talking to him.

'Morning sir, you have 45 messages' it said.

He reviewed the messages: the first was an advert with an athlete selling running shoes. The advert informed him that if he was to wear a shirt displaying the shoes, pending approval of his suitability, he could receive 0.1 credit for everyone who saw his advert and 30 credits for each purchase that resulted. He paused for a moment as the holocomputer spoke:

'You have looked at this message for two minutes, any longer and you are being unproductive. The current fine for unproductiveness is 15 credits per unproductive hour. Would you like to know more?'

'No' he said 'show me the next message'.

Once he had got to the end of his messages the holocomputer announced 'You have ten tasks to complete today to earn 100 credits.'

The rate yesterday had been 110 credits for 10 tasks. He didn't ask why the rate had changed; he knew the answer. Competition was ever present, the market was turbulent, the company was competing on a global scale and if the company and its shareholders could not earn enough money then he would be without a job as the work would be reallocated to another location where people would work at the rate offered.

He began his first task of the day. The time that had been allocated to each task was short but he could do it, he did not allow himself to get distracted as the retina scanner and the activity monitor would know if he daydreamed too long and that would just add to the pressure of getting everything done. He got through three tasks by 10.30 a.m. The holocomputer told him he was on target for the day and would receive an extra credit for superior performance. Further a little indicator highlighted how based on his current progress he was in the top 5% of workers for task efficiency that day relative to all the workers in the company. The holocomputer also told him he could take a break of 15 minutes or alternatively he could work on and earn an extra 2 credits. He thought for a minute about how time was money, but decided to take the break.

He caught the lift to the atrium level of the tower, got a coffee and walked to the benches near the tree. The only tree he knew and had seen, other than on a display. He loved the tree; it somehow made him feel peaceful. As he sat on the bench next to it he was charged a credit. The display told him, as it always did when he sat down near the tree, that the credit charge was for his taking advantage of the beauty of the tree and the investment by the company that owned it in keeping it healthy.

The time for his break ticked away; he drank his coffee and once finished he stood and made his way back to the lift. As he did so he motioned to put his coffee cup in the bin. Beep, beep, went the bin—he was about to use the wrong bin. He walked to the correct bin and put his coffee cup in it. He felt like dropping it on the floor, but he had done that before and been arrested, coffee cups had chip identifiers in them which meant the individual who had drunk from the cup and then discarded it was traceable. After depositing the coffee cup he made his way back to his workstation.

Back at his workstation he looked at the time; he was one minute late and the display told him he had been fined 1 credit. He did his tasks and at the end of each, a display indicated how efficient he was relative to others. He was not doing well, after a good start in the morning he was slipping down the league table. The display also told him that unless he boosted his efficiency he would not receive a bonus. He redoubled his efforts, efficiency was paramount. The nightly news was always reinforcing how people must be efficient lest the economy and companies fail to perform. A sustainable life could not be achieved without efficiency.

After finishing work he made his way home, helped put his children to bed and then found some time for himself. He decided to review some notes of his grandfathers. He opened the files and read them. They were written in a style of English that he was not entirely familiar with. There was an over reliance on letters in the spelling rather than letters and numbers, for example, w8 was spelled wait, 2day was spelt today. The notes outlined how there was a predominant view being put forward that money was the measure of value. Companies and even nations should compete with each other and should try to realise competitive advantage. There were some video links supporting the typed notes showing speeches from businessmen and politicians of the time repeating the message. His grandfather had put some annotations next to these videos. The basic premise of these was a questioning of what it means to be a human and whether everything should be measured in monetary terms.

He looked through the notes and came across an academic article which his grandfather had written notes on. The academic article talked about how firms should serve the underlying human need and not think in product terms. Another article discussed *how firms should invest in natural capital and continually seek to improve the efficiency of the resources they use. He thought about the tree and his own productivity. His grandfather's notes had wondered where this thinking would take society and what it meant to be a human.*

He sat back and thought that perhaps this society, his society, was where such thinking led. Companies sold solutions and there was a price on every transaction. He looked through more of his grandfather's notes. A question was written in bold letters; it asked about purpose and the implications of what it means to be human and how we define ourselves. More notes questioned how humans understand themselves and whether that understanding is formed by our relationships with all that surrounds us. Written in red, as if to accentuate importance, was a question 'will we always be Homo sapiens?'

He pressed himself upon his own understandings. He wondered about continual transparency, the visibility of one's credit balance, the only real boundary between work and non-work being time and how one maximises the latter by being efficient in the former and trying to earn credits faster than spending them. He wanted to sit under the tree, the rental tree. He felt inner peace there. He stopped reviewing his grandfather's notes. Thinking about purpose was fine, but sometimes a person can think too much. He could see that the world he lived in was an extrapolation of supposedly good ideas from before, but so what? Hadn't it always been this way?

He relaxed, smiled and thought about what could be more natural than paying for oxygen, companies investing in ecosystem services and natural resources, and companies being in the game of meeting underlying needs rather than selling products. He stood up, asked his home computer for the definition of a human: the answer came in an instant—Homo transactus economicus—brilliant, he thought, he felt comfortable. Finally, he knew exactly who he was.

Discussion and close

Notwithstanding that a reader will likely be able to pattern different theories over the content in the abridged version of the story, the key theories that informed the writing of the piece were: the notion of companies offering solutions for an underlying need as opposed to limiting their conceptions to a product offering (Levitt, 1960; Hawken et al., 1999); a monetary (credit) value being placed on natural capital; and a temporal understanding of humans (Ingold, 2011). The concept of companies selling solutions is offered via examples such as the shaving company offering information on the optimum time to shave for maximum benefit, the umbrella company being in the business of keeping an individual dry as opposed to selling umbrellas and thus charging per use, the utility company charging per use of toilet facilities with an additional service of analysing outputs and the city services charging for draining away the water that falls on the individual while he walks to work. Analogously the notion of selling services also comes through in the clothes and advertising section of this story, wherein people are offered a discount on the clothes they wish to purchase if they advertise a brand. And conversely the wealthy can afford to buy clothes with no advertising on them. The service being sold in this case is by the individual purchaser, rather than the company, with the individual receiving a discount on the purchase price of clothes in exchange for being a walking advertising hoarding for a company. As well as being another example of selling services, this piece of the narrative is also a commentary on branded clothes, wherein currently clothes brands charge a premium for their clothes and then purchasers walk around advertising that brand on their chests. For example, a logo is emblazoned across the chest. In this current context and notwithstanding other marketing arguments with regard to clothes being an expression of purchasers' values, it appears to the authors that companies are charging a premium for individuals to buy clothes who then advertise that same brand. Thus the brand is receiving a service which it is not paying for.

With regard to the monetary value of natural capital, this is captured in the narrative most explicitly by the protagonist paying credits for oxygen and being charged to sit next to a tree. Building on the notion of a monetary value being associated with ecosystem services such as oxygen, a subtext that is not developed but only alluded to in the story is that the assignation of a monetary value has led to privatisation of these services.

The temporal understanding of humanity is offered towards the end of the story when the protagonist understands that humans are currently defined as *Homo transactus economicus*, rather than *Homo sapiens*. That the story ends at this point is purposeful. It is designed as an attempt to reinforce to the reader that a key narrative throughout the story has been the placing of a monetary value on transactions. Further, in such a world, given our sense of understanding of who we are is temporal as offered by the phenotype theory (Ingold, 2011), it is likely we would perhaps not consider ourselves as *Homo sapiens* in the future portrayed by the story. But rather would consider ourselves as economic transactors and hence *Homo transactus economicus*.

Other sub-themes within the story and the value of everything being known through a medium of money are for example offered by the protagonist making a lukewarm coffee because of the active monitoring of electricity that occurs. Similarly the continual monitoring and changing of the pay rate based on a worker's efficiency relative to global comparisons. A further sub-theme behind this monitoring of pay rates and efficiency is how labour efficiency is invariably a governing thought for many organisations (Cummings, 2005). Further influences that are in the piece but only briefly referred to are that the town, Newland, is in a polar extreme of the planet, yet it is still hot. This is a narrative nod to a warming world and rising greenhouse gas levels. Also the brief discussion of a master dichotomy of consumption and production is a nod to human purpose and the writings of Marx (Ingold, 2011 citing Marx, 1930), whereby work (production) allows earnings for consumption and an individual only lives when they are consuming. Thus there is a master dichotomy that can also be termed work/life balance and one is only alive when consuming.

More current day understandings of technology and its capabilities and a relatively topical societal narrative are also alluded to. With regard to technology there is a visual electricity meter to enable active monitoring by the user, as opposed to it being locked away out of site. Retinal scanning for identification and items (things) being connected to the internet: this last aspect being made explicit when the protagonist tries to put his coffee cup in the wrong bin and an alarm sounds. A current societal narrative brought forward is the notion of credit rating of debt, a narrative which while being topical also reinforces how money is a key value indicator.

Having written the story, the authors have begun to share it with students and colleagues. Typically when sharing it with students exploratory questions are considered such as whether the world written about is a possibility and whether the levels of organisational control alluded to in the story are possible. Initial reaction from students has been concern that the world of 'Is this OK?' is possible and thus they raise a further question of what should be done. In this regard, the story has in the view of the authors been a relative success in developing students' critical faculty. It has enabled students to question natural capitalism and whether it is avoidable or inevitable and also what it means to be human and whether the economy impacts that understanding. Thus anecdotally at least the story appears to be realising its aim of facilitating students' critical faculty, albeit more considered and thorough research needs to be conducted on gauging the impact of the story on students' development of critical faculty. While critical and invariably negative discussion is raised about natural capitalism following students' reading of the story, a polemical aspect to the story is avoided by, at the end, having the protagonist be very accepting of the situation he finds himself in. The lack of concern is purposely written in order to reinforce how our understanding of ourselves and what is normal is temporal. The intention is that this enables the reader to give greater consideration to the future that is being created by and through current actions. Again anecdotally at least, students find this non-polemical stance of the story slightly disconcerting, a reaction that enables a discussion of temporal understandings and thus facilitates discussions of paradigms and current assumptions. Ultimately the temporality of understandings alludes to a challenge of our living on this planet, whereby as we live our effects keep adding to one another with the 'result that the situation for later subjects and their choices of action will be progressively different from that of the initial agent and ever more the fated product of what was done before' (Jonas, 1984: 7).

Endnote

As an endnote to this article it is worthwhile considering the terminology 'natural capitalism' and 'natural capital'. Metaphors populate and saturate our language (Mutch, 2006), further they facilitate the 'transfer of information from a relatively familiar domain (variously referred to as source or base domain, or vehicle) to a new and relatively unknown domain (usually referred to as target domain or topic)' (Tsoukas, 1991: 568). Thus they allow inferences to be made about those things we may know little about, on the basis of what we know about something else (Tsoukas, 1991, 1993). The use of metaphors in language has been likened to viruses 'which infect different discursive contexts and spread meanings' (Akerman, 2003: 432). In this regard it has been argued that metaphors can 'guide our perceptions and interpretations...and help us formulate our visions and goals' (Cornelissen *et al.*, 2008: 8), perhaps in the process connecting our experiences with our imaginations (Cornelissen *et al.*, 2008; Inns, 2002). Thus they are entwined in the relation between thought and meaning and the guidance of perception (Burr, 2003). This entwinement also results in metaphors being implied modes of behaviour (Tsoukas, 1991, 1993). Tsoukas (1991) argues that we engage in continual experience and conceptual segmentation, with language being below experience. Thus 'language is both descriptive and constitutive of reality' (Tsoukas, 1991: 568) and consequently metaphors are discursive devices that make social reality more 'palpable and comprehensible' (Tsoukas, 1991: 571) than it might otherwise be. Consequently metaphors both reflect and influence action (Burr, 2003; Ford and Ford, 1995; Lakoff and Johnson, 1980; Tsoukas, 1991, 1993). As such while metaphors can be a short hand towards guiding actions, at the same time they can hide, obscure or realise ideological distortions (for example see; Akerman, 2003; Audebrand, 2010; Mutch, 2006; Oswick *et al.*, 2002; Tinker, 1986; Tsoukas, 1991, 1993) in the movement and application of principles from the base domain to target domain.

Akerman (2003) argues that the term 'natural capital', and by extension 'natural capitalism', is one such distortion. Akerman (2003) highlights how the introduction of the concept of natural capital is a success particularly because of the properties of the term as a metaphor; in as much as the terminology invites 'the audience to approach the relationship between nature and economy in a new way with familiar economic terms' (Akerman, 2003: 436), the modus operandi of metaphors. Further Akerman (2003) highlights that the term natural capital moves nature from being considered as a passive store towards something that is actively managed, as nature is now an asset not just a store. This movement from store to asset, it is argued, facilitates the monetisation of nature and its consideration in ahistorical, decontextual and economic terms only (Akerman, 2003). Referring back to the story, Akerman's (2003) argument is brought forward wherein the consideration of natural capital in economic terms becomes an accepted norm. Thus a monetary charge is taken for breathing oxygen and sitting near a tree. Consequently, a partial aim of the story is to highlight that while a concept such as natural capitalism might be acceptable within the current context, the bridge of current acceptability for the concept facilitated by the metaphor of natural capitalism has within it the seeds of future consequences that are challenging when viewed from our current context.

References

Akerman, M. (2003), 'What Does "Natural Capital" Do? The Role of Metaphor in Economic Understanding of the Environment', *Environmental Values*, 12(4): 431-448.

Audebrand, L.K. (2010), 'Sustainability in Strategic Management Education: The Quest for New Root Metaphors', *Academy of Management Learning & Education*, 9(3): 413-428.

Barter, N., Houghton, L., Eyley, J. & Renn, E. (2013), *Is this okay? An exploration of extremes*, Available at www.isthisokay.com.

Burr, V. (2003), *Social constructionism*, Routledge, London.

Cornelissen, J.P., Oswick, C., Christensen, L.T. and Phillips N. (2008), 'Metaphor in organizational research: Context, modalities and implications for research—Introduction', *Organization Studies*, 29(1):7–22.

Costanza, R., d'Arge, R., De Groot, R., Farber, S., Grasso, M., Hannon, B., Limburg, K., Naeem, S., O'Neill, R.V., Paruelo, J., Raskin, R. G., Sutton, P. and Van den Belt, M. (1997), 'The value of the world's ecosystem services and natural capital', *Nature*, 387 (May): 253-260.

Cummings, S. (2005), *Recreating Strategy*, Sage, London.

Ford, J.D. and Ford, L.W. (1995), 'The Role of Conversations in producing Intentional change in Organisations', *Academy of Management Review*, 20(3): 541-570.

Hawken, P., Lovins, A.B. and Lovins, L.H. (1999), 'A Road Map for Natural Capitalism', *Harvard Business Review*, May-June: 145-148.

Hoover, S. (2012), 'The Case for Graphic Novels', *Communications in Information Literacy*, 5(2), Retrieved from www.eduscapes.com/instruction/articles/hoover.pdf.

Ingold, T. (2001), *The Perception of the Environment*, Routledge, Abingdon.

Ingold, T. (2011), *Being Alive: Essays on Movement, Knowledge and Description*, Routledge, Abingdon.

Inns, D. (2002), 'Metaphor in the Literature of Organizational Analysis: A Preliminary Taxonomy and a Glimpse at a Humanities-Based Perspective', *Organization*, 9: 305-330.

Jonas, H. (1984), *The Imperative of Responsibility*, The University of Chicago Press, Chicago.

Lakoff, G. and Johnson, M. (1980), *Metaphors We Live By*, University of Chicago Press, Chicago.

Levitt, T. (1960), 'Marketing Myopia', *Harvard Business Review*, July-August: 138-149.

Marx, K. (1930), *Capital*, 1, translation Paul E. and Paul, C. Dent, London.

Mezirow, J. (1994), 'Understanding Transformation Theory', *Adult Education Quarterly*, 44: 222-232.

Mutch, A. (2006), 'Organization theory and military metaphor: Time for a reappraisal?' *Organization*, 13(6): 751-769.

Oswick, C., Keenoy, T. and Grant, D. (2002), 'Metaphor and analogical reasoning in organization theory: Beyond orthodoxy', *Academy of Management Review*, 27(2): 294-303.

Porritt, J. (2006), *Capitalism as if the World Matters*, Earthscan, London.

Tinker, T. (1986), 'Metaphor or reification: are radical humanists really libertarian anarchists?' *Journal of Management Studies*, 23(4): 363-386.

Tsoukas, H. (1991), 'The Missing link: A Transformational View of Metaphors in Organizational Science', *Academy of Management Review*, 16(3): 566-585.

Tsoukas, H. (1993), 'Analogical Reasoning and Knowledge Generation in Organization Theory', *Organization Studies*, 14: 323-346.

Weiler, A. (2004), 'Information-Seeking Behavior in Generation Y Students : Motivation, Critical Thinking, and Learning Theory', *The Journal of Academic Librarianship*, 31(1): 46-53.

The Quest Games

A Tale of Career Advancement

Candice Harris, Katherine Ravenswood and Barbara Myers

AUT University, New Zealand

This article explores the individual experiences and perceptions of career progression in a large public organisation. The research comprised 32 in-depth interviews with employees across one organisation. We use a narrative inquiry approach to analyse individuals' stories and present the findings of the research in the form of a fictional story, 'The Quest Games'. We argue that the power of the fictional story approach in this article on career advancement is twofold. First, the lived reality of nuances in promotion processes and career paths which are underscored by organisational hierarchies, power structures and networks are illustrated. Second, we engage the reader at an individual level by inviting her or him to reflect on and resonate with their own stories of career progression.

- Careers
- Advancement
- Women
- Narrative inquiry
- Storytelling
- Organisations
- Networks
- Meritocracy

Candice Harris is an Associate Professor in Management at AUT University. She teaches management and supervises postgraduate students working in the fields of careers and management. Her main areas of research are career development, gender issues in management, discourses of work, and qualitative and critical approaches to research.

Faculty of Business & Law, AUT University, Private Bag 92006, Auckland 1142, New Zealand

candice.harris@aut.ac.nz

Katherine Ravenswood is a senior lecturer in the Department of Management at AUT University. Katherine teaches management, employment relations, HRM and organisational behaviour. Her current research interests include employee voice, aged care, family friendly policy and parental leave, and women and diversity at work.

Faculty of Business & Law, AUT University, Private Bag 92006, Auckland 1142, New Zealand.

kravensw@aut.ac.nz

Barbara Myers is a senior lecturer in human resource management, international human resource management, careers and personal and professional development in the Department of Management at AUT University. Barbara teaches on undergraduate and postgraduate programmes and her current research interests include self-initiated expatriation, older workers, gender, international careers and work (paid and unpaid).

Faculty of Business & Law, AUT University, Private Bag 92006, Auckland 1142, New Zealand

Barbara.myers@aut.ac.nz

N THIS ARTICLE WE DRAW on the individual stories of women and men in a large public organisation. These narratives (individual stories) are the basis for the creation of a fictional 'Quest Games' story. We draw on Crossley (2000) and McCormick (2004) who suggest the writing of a story as a way of analysing, interpreting and presenting final themes. In 'storying the stories' (McCormick 2004), practices and regimes that are frequently invisible in organisations are able to be illustrated (Acker 2006; Simpson and Lewis 2007; Sandina 2007, Myers 2011).

We begin this article with our fictional story 'The Quest Games' cognisant of a number of issues and themes that are implicit in the story. This is followed by an outline of the research approach and process. Both of these sections give consideration to 'narrative inquiry' as an appropriate methodology for this research study. The subsequent section contains an extensive discussion on careers within a particular organisational context. This discussion highlights key factors that impede organisational advancement with a more specific focus on deconstructing notions of organisational meritocracy, networks and diverse values systems. Finally we consider the validity of 'storytelling' as a way to reflect the reality of participant stories and experiences in a meaningful way, and as a way for readers to make sense of key issues and themes.

Our story: The Quest Games

Today it starts. On this day, the thirtieth day of the fourth month, the 135th year of the Quest begins. Although less than 30 players enter the Quest each year, it is shared by all in Tremus as the premier event. Folklore has it that the Quest has been part of Tremus tradition for over a century now.

Our story features three players: Calin, from Central; Winart, from the West; and Epsilon from the East. While each player has their own unique mix of excitement, anticipation, and confidence, our three players consider themselves ready for the contest. So let us begin ladies and gentlemen. Who has what it takes to win the Quest and enter the Cocerna?

Tremus: a tale of three cities

Welcome to Tremus, a city of 300,000 people spread over three regions. Our residents of the Central region are known as Centrions, those in the East are Easters, and Westalas are from the West. Xenons are a group that migrate between the three regions, depending on where the opportunities related to work, leisure, nature or health lie.

The governing council of Tremus, the Cocerna, comprises 100 people. The Cocerna has an inner sanctum of council leaders who oversee the three regions, and an outer core of region and industry experts who advise the inner sanctum on their specific region. Occasionally, newcomers are recruited from outside Tremus to the outer core of the council as positions become vacant.

Entry to the Cocerna is through the annual Quest games. Mystery surrounds the exact number of places available each year under 'Council Quest' rules. Any citizen except Xenons can enter the annual quest. Players need to have Carriage *(a collection of various assets) before embarking on the quest. It can take years to get Carriage through innovation and adding value to industry, although assets, established from previous achievements and recognition in other cities, can be included when assessing an individual's level of Carriage.*

I'm going to let you into a secret now: the judges of the Quest, Potentates, *are already Cocerna members. They prefer to keep things more or less stable so they are not too perturbed by the high percentage of Centrions on the Cocerna. Residents of Tremus widely believe that the activities of Central are more highly regarded than those of the West or the East.*

Now you should know there are three different types of assets that give a player carriage: industry earnings, influence, and networks that players build over the years. I hear that for this year's assets 'industry earnings' reign supreme. If you have most of these as your assets you are in with a good chance of winning a seat on the Cocerna. Some 'influence' will help, as will good 'networks', but it is industry earnings that will really advantage players.

Choose your guardians carefully! These are the people who will lobby on your behalf. You need to be very savvy in your choice of guardian and work out who does what, and who will reward you freely without demanding payback.

Can you hear that? It's the cheering crowd! Now, enough of these rumours and idle chatter, let's go and see who the players are this year.

Players: the 135th year of the Quest

Calin *from Central enters the Quest to the roaring of the crowd and heralding of trumpets. There's no doubt of Centrions' respect for those who show ambition and drive, and they certainly are proud that Centrions dominate the Cocerna with 65% of membership. Centrion guardians even favour their own in granting assets and advice. Central is our most compact region which has been heavily built up. With a mix of new and older residents (Centrions), this region holds fast to tradition, particularly traditions of ascent to the Cocerna (Tremus's governing council). Some* Centrions *have family histories in the region that span several generations. Others have moved in over the last 30 years, attracted from other regions by the economic development opportunities Tremus offers. Central has the strongest relationship with the Cocerna, with the most citizens on the council out of all three regions. However, Central leaders are excited by the newer industries developing in the West region and are working actively to develop closer relations with those in the West.*

Anyway, back to up-and-coming Calin who is a newer citizen of Central, having moved there only five years ago with a partner and two children. Calin is a truly cosmopolitan citizen who arrived with assets earned in other cities. Calin is one of the Quest favourites and is very well connected. Calin works in the media and Calin's partner works in finance. These are key industries in Central. Calin is well placed having secured Dorphus as a guardian. You will have heard of Dorphus who has directorships in the same media organisation as Calin, as well as the finance and banking industries. On top of this, Dorphus has previously competed in the Quest and is well-appraised of the Quest rules, having also served as a Quest Potentate several times. Calin keeps up with trends in the Quest and in Tremus, and has seen a shift in the currency of Quest assets over the last five years. Tremus has aligned itself more with the rules of other cities, so that Carriage has become more and more important in the Quest and the emphasis is now on the assets earned since Carriage had been awarded. Calin seems quite confident with the assets earned from other cities which are particularly prized by Cocerna as proof of Calin's success.

Look, here comes Winart. Hear that rowdy crowd cheer Winart onto the stage. I can see that Winart's putting on a brave face. I heard that Winart's a bit apprehensive seeing as not many Westalas have made it through to the Cocerna in recent years. The West has a small population of 50,000. It is an exciting, newer region known for new technology industries. Westalas are forging stronger relationships with Central and Centrion Cocerna members are slowly changing and can see that the West is driving innovation and growth in Tremus. These Centrion members can see the potential value of having more Westalas on the Cocerna—it could be Winart's lucky year.

Let me tell you about Winart. Winart is a software engineer for a medical robotics company and is single. Winart has not played in the Quest before, but has been quietly asking around and realises that there is a lot more to the Quest than you can see. I heard on the grapevine that Winart would rather take a year or two longer to develop some good Guardian relationships from Central, and the West, but Winart's friends and colleagues have been putting pressure on Winart to enter for the West. Clearly Winart has bowed to those demands. Can Winart make it through the whole six weeks of the Quest, I wonder?

The crowd has gone quiet. Oh, there's Epsilon, a well-respected senior carer of the birlas from the East. The East has a long tradition of community and caring for the land and the birlas (bird creatures whose behaviour forewarns weather patterns enabling locals to protect the crops). Easters take great pride in this, and consider it to be important work for their own community and also for those of us from the West and Central. The East is sparsely populated, and with its focus on agriculture and the birlas, it is a spacious, leafy and comfortable place to live. In the past, agriculture and birlas have been greatly respected by people outside of the East, but recently there's been some disquiet in the East. Easters feel that their own ways and work are overlooked in favour of the strong commercial industries of Central and the fast growing new technology industries of the West. Not everyone's convinced that Easters should enter the Quest on the terms of the Centrion-dominated Cocerna. Until the rules change and the assets that Easters earn are seen for their true worth, then some Easters don't want a bar of the Quest. Poor Epsilon, it's a tricky position to be in and you can guarantee that if Epsilon does not win the Cocerna position it will be because Epsilon just did not meet Quest standards.

Enough doom and gloom. Could this be the year for the East? Epsilon's got a point to prove and has decided to enter the quest to prove that Easters' work is just as important as that done by citizens of Central and the West. Epsilon has found a guardian that is well connected with Central and the West. The guardian is helping out with advice on how to acquire assets. That way, although networks are Epsilon's strength, Epsilon may also manage to claim some industry earnings and influence.

This is almost unprecedented. Things are looking up for Easters this year and it seems possible that there might be a greater number of Easters on the Potentate!

Thus it might be a good year for the Easters, but they have a very mixed record of success. Then there are the Westalas, who are in hot demand by Central who value their emerging and innovative industries. Easters in general may not have enough knowledge and experience of the Quest, and if Guardians and the Potentate are backing the West almost as much as Central, what will that mean for Easters? There is some excitement, anticipation and just a little frustration in the East and West.

So, we ask you, the audience!

Who will win the Quest this year?

Who do you support? Epsilon, Calin or Winart?

Do you have your own Quest story?

Background to 'The Quest Games' story

The development of the 'Quest Games' narrative was undertaken as a way of illustrating common themes that resonate across different organisational contexts and individual experiences. These themes were drawn from a research project conducted in 2011–2012. The overall aim of this research project was to examine promotion processes and outcomes in a university context. More specifically, we set out to assess the perceptions and experiences of promotion processes (from the 'invitation to apply' stage to the promotion 'decision outcome' stage) and identify any perceived barriers to the career success of academic staff and in particular female academic staff.

We decided to present the findings in a generic narrative to draw attention to the universality of the themes regarding these women's experiences and how women and other minority groups are often marginalised and silenced in organisational power structures and processes (Acker 2006).

Research approach

Methodologically, the research was driven by a qualitative, interpretive research approach. An interpretive epistemology assumes that social meanings are created which implies individuals may understand social reality differently, producing different meanings and analyses (Hesse-Biber and Leavy 2006). A narrative inquiry framework was chosen as we concur with Bruner (1986, 1987), who argues that narrative is a valid medium for exploring and thinking in a different way to a positivist approach. Bruner (1987) suggests that a narrative approach draws on memory, both consciously and unconsciously, in an interpretive process. Sarbin (1986) and Weick (1995) also argue that narrative is a rich metaphor for sense making while Polkinghorne (1988) suggests that analysis of 'narrative knowing' facilitates 'making meaning' and is fundamental to understanding human experience especially aspects of organisational inequalities (Acker, 2006).

Consistent within the narrative inquiry framework, we drew on both the 'analysis of narrative' and the 'narrative analysis' approaches to analyse and present data (Clandinin and Connelly, 2000; Mishler, 1995; Polkinghorne, 1995). While these approaches are discussed more fully in the following section the latter approach (narrative analysis) allowed the authors an opportunity to be more flexible and creative in the analysis of data via the fictional story, thus affording an opportunity to write and present findings in a different way (Bold, 2012).

This research study explores individual experiences and perceptions of career progression in a university setting. Ethical approval was obtained for the study from the university ethics committee and the principal research instrument used in this study was the in-depth, semi-structured interview which was the primary source of data for the research.

The participants were drawn from a population of 899 academic staff and within that a target group of senior lecturers and associate professors. The aim was to achieve a sample that varied in age, gender and ethnicity where possible across all faculties of the university, consequently women and male colleagues were interviewed. The number of participants was guided by the exploratory nature of the study and the scope of the research project, and overall 32 participants were interviewed which was deemed sufficient to gain a range of views from staff across different faculties.

The interviews were analysed qualitatively and informed by constructs in the extant literature. The analytical process drew on Braun and Clarke's (2006) six-step process and the 'analysis of narrative' approach (Polkinghorne, 1995). This inductive process generated some common trends across the whole sample as well some different trends and experiences for female participants compared with male participants.

During the analytical process the notion of promotion processes being a type of 'game' emerged. For example, participants identified the importance of having a game plan and the competitive nature of promotion processes as key themes. Several women participants also acknowledged their inability to play the promotion game as they believed the rules did not recognise or value the activities that they enjoyed and excelled in. Thus the analogy of *The Hunger Games* seemed an appropriate and timely model to draw on as it captured the competitive aspect of many of the stories.

The writing of the fictional story 'The Quest Games' follows the 'narrative analysis' approach where researchers gather, analyse, re-construct and re-present data in a single story (Clandinin and Connelly 2000; Mishler 1995). Bold (2012: 4) asserts that fictional story writing is a way of 'collating and analysing a set of data into a coherent, valid, reliable and accessible piece that represents the whole data set.' The authors decided to create a fictional story on career advancement rather than a factual narrative as the generic aspect of a fictional story reaches out beyond the immediate research context. For example during the analytical process three key groups were identified. These were older females, males and younger females. The authors did not wish to initially disclose these groups or the specific university setting of the research as they believed the findings were relevant to a wider organisational context. Writing a fictional story also affords the participants a high level of confidentiality and anonymity which is particularly important when conducting research in a known environment. Finally the fictional story was employed as it potentially embraces a wider audience and is more compelling as it creates less distance and formality between the writer and the reader. This ensures that the themes and messages of the story are more 'readable, accessible, engaging, interesting and useful' to a greater range of readers.[1]

Czarniawaska (2004) suggests that the legitimacy of a fictional story is gained from the response of the reader and that trustworthiness, plausibility and criticality in the fictional story is established if it facilitates 'reader reflection' on their own experiences as the story unfolds. Thus the Quest story concludes with an exhortation to the audience inviting them not only to engage in the Quest by declaring their sympathies and identifying a possible winner, but also to consider their own history of Quest-type game experiences.

Discussion

Positioning of women in universities

Structural imbalances are reflected in our story by the Central region where the majority of Tremus citizens are domiciled. Central have also dominated the Council Quest for many years and as a consequence they generally hold a majority of the seats on the governing council, the Cocerna. While the population in the West and East increases, Central is still dominant in terms of leadership. Inequities were further exacerbated as most Quest Guardians and Potentates are from Central and Quest players need to be sponsored by a Guardian to gain entry to the Quest. Research shows that in many countries, the representation of women in senior academic positions is low (Maranto and Griffin 2011). Recent Australian research found similar patterns: at early lecturer level over 50% of positions are held by women, whereas associate professor and professorial positions are predominantly held by men. This is despite increasing participation of women as academics in universities (Strachan *et al.* 2011). A greater percentage of women in senior positions is perceived to have an impact on managerial culture and therefore improve opportunities for other women (Browning 2008; Monroe *et al.* 2008). There is considerable research that also points to the role of mentors and sponsors in women's advancement and that is discussed in more detail elsewhere (see for example, Baker 2010; Harris *et al.* 2013; Monroe *et al.* 2008; Sherman *et al.* 2010; van den Brink *et al.* 2010).

---

1 *The Journal of Corporate Citizenship* 'Homepage', www.greenleaf-publishing.com/default .asp?ContentID=16, accessed 30 October 2012.

Under Council Quest rules, Xenons (migrant group) are not eligible to play in the Quest. This is an example of the lack of recognition of the impact of family and childbearing on academic careers (Rhoton 2011; Webster 2010). Often part-time permanent staff are excluded from promotion criteria: the majority of Australian universities did not allow part-time permanent academics to apply for promotion. This has significant impact on women who form the majority of part-time academic staff (Winchester *et al.* 2006). The absence of Xenons from the story of the Quest games reflects their effective absence from academic 'careers'.

Advancement through 'meritocracy'

A barrier to women's academic promotion is policy based on meritocracy (van den Brink and Benschop 2012a; Webster 2010). Often policies and practices based on merit for certain criteria actually create inequalities because of the differences in ways of working between men and women (Webster 2010). Such barriers are picked up in our story by the fact that most Quest Guardians and Potentates are from Central and most Cocerna members have histories in terms of industry experience similar to those from Central. This means that 'merit' or what counts as carriage is defined and judged by Centrions. Given that the majority of senior university positions are held by men (Strachan *et al.* 2011), it is most likely that university promotion committees are also dominated by senior male academics (Maranto and Griffin 2011). Many of these barriers are not caused by overt discrimination, but by unconscious attitudes towards work organisation and the value of work performed by men and women (Baker 2009; Monroe *et al.* 2008). In our story, while the Council Quest is advertised as open to all, Central players have a definite advantage due to the valuing by the Cocerna of Central's key industries.

There is no exact formula for the number and type of assets required for success, therefore there are considerable 'urban myths' covertly shared about the value of assets in achieving Quest success. Previous Quest winners, Guardians and especially Potentates all keep Quest strategies fairly close to themselves, hence understanding successful Quest strategy often remains cloaked in mystery. The precise strategies of Quest winners and Cocerna members are rarely declared or publicised. The lack of transparency can work to both increase the desirability of the Quest, as well as the nerves of potential and actual Quest players! Women benefit from greater transparency because it encourages accountability and because 'bias is more likely to occur when assessments are based on obscure criteria and the process of evaluation kept confidential' (van Den Brink *et al.* 2010: 1459). Because Cocerna membership consists of 65% of those from Central, there is less understanding and 'whispers' in the East or West about how players actually won positions in the Council Quest. Although there is a governing Council Quest policy, how it is applied is more fluid and less transparent, due to the unique composition of Quest Potentates Groups each year.

Gendered ideas of career paths and academic success are a considerable barrier to women's career advancement. Those from Central gain Carriage faster than those in the East. The West has the greatest numbers of residents who gain Carriage at an earlier age in a former region and then migrated to the West. Council Potentates understand Carriage and assets gained in Central to a greater degree than Carriage and assets gained in the West or East. The industries in the West have not fully developed and their potential is as yet undetermined, so the Cocerna is still debating how value will be attributed to assets from this region.

That Central players possess more industry earnings than other players captures the notion that women's career advancement is potentially disadvantaged in organisational cultures that place most emphasis on research publications as evidence of merit for promotion. Men generally have had greater numbers of publications, and therefore greater success in academic promotion particularly where research publications take precedence over other contributions to the organisation (Webster 2010). The number of publications may correlate to the hours of work by both men and women. One impact on the number of publications is the hours spent in other roles: for example, women often have higher teaching loads, which disadvantages them through less time to devote to research and publications (Baker, 2010). Furthermore, men report working longer hours than women, and often with lower perceptions of negative impact on their health and family life (Baker, 2010; Monroe et al., 2008; Webster, 2010).

Some of the explanations for why men may publish more than women centre on the unspoken expectations for women in universities. For example, women tend to be more involved in teaching and 'carework', such as pastoral care of students and service which is not valued as much in promotion processes as research publications (Monroe et al. 2008; Sherman et al. 2011). Some research indicates that when the amount of time spent teaching was included as evidence of merit as well as the degree of research specialisation and non-refereed publications, there was little difference between men and women (Leahy 2006, 2007). Compounding any gendered disadvantage, women's and men's similar achievements are evaluated differently with, for example, men's service contributions assessed more highly than women's (Nakhaie 2007; van der Brink et al. 2010; van den Brink and Benschop 2012b). Players from the West and the East tend to hold a similar number of Quest assets to those held by Central players, but less of the coveted industry earnings, and higher degrees of influence and networks.

Monroe et al. (2008: 220) suggest that, although women know that service does not have the same recognition, rewards and career prospects as research, they engage in it anyway because they recognise that 'such positions enabled them to open things up for other women'. In the Quest story, 'influence' is valued less than 'industry earnings', although this is a moving relativity and some degree of influence is necessary to improve the likelihood of winning a Cocerna position. The assets 'industry earnings' correlate to research publications, and 'influence' relate to academic service and industry connections in academia. Despite the lack of value attached to networks, East and West players enjoy building networks, which are created more as a community. Networks in our Quest Games refer to 'care work' or relationship building and support. Indeed, those from the West and East are perceived to be better at relationship tasks. In academia there is also an expectation among colleagues and academic managers that women will take care of relationship building and the 'nurturing and housekeeping side of academic life' (Sherman *et al.* 2010). This again potentially disadvantages women in the academic career game.

A counterpoint to the importance of Carriage and the value of assets in the Council Quest is the lack of value for unpaid work and sustainability tasks (birlas) in the Council Quest. While care for birlas does not count for Council Quest, some are not bothered by this as they love caring for birlas and do it anyway. Women often perceive motherhood to have a huge impact on their academic career because the amount of work required to be successful is only possible without children or other responsibilities (Baker 2010). Family is perceived by some to be invisible in academia and having children slows academic careers down, a finding that has also been reported by men who share childcare and domestic work with their partners (Baker 2010). Childless, single women perceived that they have a distinct advantage in terms of time to give to work (Baker 2009). Some women who prioritise their work over family choose this unwillingly but in recognition that to prioritise family would be at the cost of promotion (Webster 2010). In our story new birlas were seen as a disadvantage for Questing in a specific time period. As birlas care made Council Questing more challenging, some hid their birlas work, worried about the judgements that would be made about it. As mentioned earlier, there are several barriers potentially to women's career advancement in academia, and one of these is the lack of recognition of the impact of external roles. For example, traditional career paths are modelled on full-time work with no career breaks.

Traditional career paths are not an option for all, such as those who care for the birlas. However, rather than recognising gendered systems and practices of the university and academia, any failure of a woman to advance is seen to be because of some fault in her performance or person (Rhoton 2011). The Quest Games is deliberately presented as a non-gendered story in order to highlight the faults in the systems and practices of career progression in universities rather than specific attributes of individuals. It reveals the subtle rules, expectations and biases that are not explicitly acknowledged in a meritocracy. The Easters continue to carry out important work caring for birlas, yet this work is not recognised much in the Quest. Further, those from the West and East who do not succeed are often demoralised and embarrassed and do not enter the games again for some time, if at all, blaming some failing or inadequacy in their self.

Network support for advancement

Informal networks are important for mentoring, information gathering and decision making in the academic appointments process and also in formal research collaborations. A lack of formal networks can impact negatively on women's career advancement particularly in universities or disciplines where men dominate (Maranto and Griffin 2011). In the Quest story players from Central were better supported by Guardians and former players for the Quest. Players from the West and East often have a more isolated journey in preparing for the Council Quest. Some players from the East and West had received advice from earlier Council Quest players, but they still had fewer people to seek advice from compared to players from Central. Many on the Cocerna with industry experience relevant to those from East and West had been appointed in from other cities, thus were not as 'known' compared to the strong intergenerational networks that existed in Central. This relates to differences in academia in how, for example, a discipline dominated by men may be given greater weight or value by a promotion committee than a discipline dominated by women. Networks within universities can aid women's career advancement through increased visibility and understanding of more kinds or research. Strong networks also disseminate important, unspoken organisational knowledge which can be essential for successful promotion (Maranto and Griffin 2011).

Research suggests that women often have less confidence in their intelligence and ability than men (Baker 2010). Thus it is understandable that they are not as confident in highlighting their capabilities in promotion (Browning 2008; Probert 2005) although they often feel more positive about their academic career when they know they have the support of management (Webster 2010). In the Quest story most successful players from the West in recent times had enjoyed good support from strong Guardians who had reached out from Central to advise on Quest strategy. Guardians, however, did not gift assets to West players to the same extent that they did to Central players.

Conclusion

We have used fictional story writing as a tool to explore the 'promotion' experiences of 32 academic staff. The key issues that arose are particularly strong because they come from the experiences of individuals across different faculties and disciplines in the university. The themes that emerged from the study related to assumptions and understandings of meritocracy, personal and professional networks, and the differing value perceived to be assigned to different types of academic work.

Guidelines regarding merit in a variety of academic areas were perceived by participants to not always align with the actual performance that was awarded promotion. More precisely some perceived there to be a focus on research outputs, viewed as a largely individual pursuit, in comparison to service to both organisational and external community stakeholders, and teaching.

The availability and use of networks was crucial to success in promotion. University-wide networks increased the sources and types of information that people receive about promotion, the 'nuances' of what is expected and rewarded, which was not clear in formal promotion processes and guidelines. These networks especially informed and encouraged women in the promotion process.

In addition to presenting our findings in an engaging and novel way (*JCC* homepage, see footnote above; Bold, 2012), fictional story writing facilitates a number of our research agendas. First it protects research participants. Second it offers a vehicle to explore the reality that sits beneath the veneer of 'best practice' academic promotion processes. Third it gives a voice to groups who are marginalised and silenced in the rational and managerialist culture of the modern day entrepreneurial university (Simpson and Lewis 2007; Sandina 2007; Myers 2011). Finally fictional story writing in the context of this specific research project provides a useful tool for teaching organisational culture, career advancement and 'lived' gender issues as they are played out in the hierarchies, power structures and networks of organisational life.

We concur with Crang and Crook (2007) that all research, encompassing all methodological approaches, is impacted by the researcher, especially when people, relationships and experiences are examined. When employing a narrative framework, the concepts of validity, reliability and replicability are reconfigured. Bold (2012) argues that validity is established if the story has relevance to the lives of research participants, replicability is established if the audience reading the stories relate them to other stories they are aware of, and reliability is established if readers identify with aspects of the stories in their own professional lives.

In 'storying' the individual participant stories, we acknowledge principles drawn from 'feminism, postmodernism and qualitative research' (McCormick 2004: 220), and argue that 'narrative inquiry' is an appropriate framework for this research, thus echoing the views of Connelly and Clandinin (1994: 4046) that 'One of the best ways to study human beings is to come to grips with the "storied nature of human beings"'.

References

Acker, J. (2006) 'Inequality Regimes: Gender, Class and Race in Organizations', *Gender & Society* 20.4: 441-464.

Baker, M. (2009) 'Gender, academia and the managerial university', *New Zealand Sociology* 24.1: 24-48.

Baker, M. (2010) 'Career confidence and gendered expectations of academic promotion', *Journal of Sociology* 46.3: 317-334.

Bold, C. (2012) *Using Narrative in Research* (London: Sage Publications).

Braun, V. and V. Clarke (2006) 'Using thematic analysis in psychology', *Qualitative Research in Psychology* 3: 77-101.

Browning, L. (2008) 'Leading women: The positive impact of women and leadership programs', in S. Grenz, B. Kortendiek, M. Kriszio, and A. Löther (eds.), *Gender Equality Programmes in Higher Education. International Perspectives* (Wiesbaden, Germany: VS Verlag): 179-191.

Bruner, J. (1986) *Actual minds, possible worlds* (Cambridge, MA: Harvard University Press).

Bruner, J. (1987) 'Life as narrative', *Social research* 1.1:11-32.

Clandinin, D. J. and M. Connelly (2000) *Narrative inquiry: Experience and story in qualitative research* (San Francisco: Jossey-Bass).

Connelly, F.M. and D.J. Clandinin (1994) 'Narrative Inquiry', in T. Husen and T.N. Postlethwaite (eds.), *The International Encyclopaedia of Education Volume 7*, second edition (Oxford: Pergamon Press): 4046-4051.

Crang, M. and I. Crook (2007) *Doing Ethnographies* (London: Sage).

Crossley, M. (2000) *Introducing narrative psychology: Self, trauma and the construction of meaning* (Philadephia, PA: Open University Press).

Czarniawska, B. (2004) *Narratives in Social Science Research. Introducing Qualitative Methods* (Thousand Oaks, CA: Sage publications).

Harris, C., Ravenswood, K. & Myers, B. (2013) Glass slippers, Holy Grails and Ivory Towers: gender and advancement in academia, *Labour & Industry: a journal of the social and economic relations of work* 23.3: 231-244

Hesse-Biber, S.N. and S.I. Leberman (2006) *The Practice of Qualitative Research* (Thousand Oaks, CA: Sage).

Leahey, E. (2006) 'Gender Differences in Productivity', *Gender & Society* 20.6: 754-780.

Leahey, E. (2007) 'Not by productivity alone: How visibility and specialization contribute to academic earnings', *American Sociological Review* 72.4: 533-561.

Maranto, C. L., and A.E. Griffin (2011) 'The antecedents of a "chilly climate" for women faculty in higher education', *Human Relations* 64.2: 139-159.

McCormack, C. (2004) 'Storying stories: a narrative approach to in-depth interview conversations', *International Journal of Social Research Methodology* 7.3: 219-236.

Mishler, E. G. (1995) 'Models of Narrative Analysis: A Typology', *Journal of Narrative and Life History* 5.2: 87–123.

Monroe, K., S. Ozyurt, T. Wrigley, and A. Alexander (2008) 'Gender equality in Academia: Bad news from the trenches, and some possible solutions', *Perspectives on Politics* 6.2: 215-233.

Myers, B. (2011) 'Self Initiated Expatriation (SIE) in older women: Exploring a different terrain' *Women's Studies Journal* 251.2: 102-107.

Nakhaie, M. R. (2007) 'Universalism, ascription and academic rank: Canadian Professors, 1987-2000*', *The Canadian Review of Sociology* 44.3: 361-386.

Polkinghorne, D. E. (1988) *Narrative Knowing and the Human Sciences* (Albany, NY: State University of New York Press).

Polkinghorne, D. E. (1995) 'Narrative configuration in qualitative analysis', *Qualitative Studies in Education* 8.1: 5-23.

Probert, B. (2005) '"I just couldn't fit it in": Gender and unequal outcomes in academic careers', *Gender, Work & Organization* 12.1: 50-72.

Rhoton, L. A. (2011) 'Distancing as a gendered barrier', *Gender & Society* 25.6: 696-716.

Sandina, L. (2007) 'Relating process: Accounts of influence in the life history interview', *Journal of Visual Arts Practice* 6.3: 191-197.

Sarbin, T. R. (1986) 'The Narrative as a Root Metaphor for psychology', in T.R. Sarbin (ed.), *Narrative psychology. The Storied Nature of Human Conduct* (London: Praeger): 3-21.

Sherman, W. H., Beaty, D. M., Crum, K. S., and Peters, A. (2010) 'Unwritten: young women faculty in educational leadership', *Journal of Educational Administration* 48(6), 741-754.

Simpson, R. and Lewis, P. (2007) *Voice, visibility and the gendering of organizations* (New York: Palgrave MacMillan).

Strachan, G., K. Broadbent, G. Whitehouse, D. Peetz, R. May, C. Kynaston, E. Ruckley and J. Bailey (2011) 'Australian Universities—Where are the women?', paper presented at *Dialogue Downunder, the 25th AIRAANZ Conference*, Auckland, New Zealand, 2–4 February 2011.

van den Brink, M., and Y. Benschop (2012a) 'Gender practices in the construction of academic excellence: Sheep with five legs', *Organization* 19.4: 507-524.

van den Brink, M., and Y. Benschop (2012b) 'Slaying the seven-headed dragon: The quest for gender change in academia', *Gender, Work & Organization* 19.1: 71-92.

van den Brink, M., Y. Benschop and W. Jansen (2010) 'Transparency in academic recruitment: A problematic tool for gender equality?', *Organization Studies* 31.11: 1459-1483.

Webster, J. (2010) *Women academics: Tensions between the workplace and the personal and professional selves: a thesis presented in partial fulfilment of the requirements for the degree of Master of Education in Adult Education* (Massey University, Palmerston North, New Zealand). Retrieved 17 January 2012 from www.mro.massey.ac.nz/handle/10179/1799.

Weick, K. E. (1995) *Sensemaking in Organizations* (Thousand Oaks, CA: Sage Publications, Inc).

Winchester, H., S. Lorenzo, L. Browning and C. Chesterman (2006) 'Academic women's promotions in Australian universities', *Employee Relations* 28.6: 505–522.

Undermining the Corporate Citizen

An Academic Story[*]

Suzanne Ryan
University of Newcastle, Australia

James Guthrie
Macquarie University, Australia and Bologna University, Italy

Employing a story to present the results of a longitudinal study of 21 Australian business academics, the paper provides insight into the life of a mythical academic, Bill, and his responses to a changing academic environment during the period 2002 to 2008. A storytelling method is employed as a means to encourage the reader's identification with Bill's story and, using a broad Habermasian lens on institutional change, to question the degree to which Bill's values were colonised by the changes. In addition to further understanding of the impacts of institutional change on academic values and identity, the paper's contribution lies in its novel approach to presenting research findings in a way that allows the interpretation to connect reader and subject on a personal level.

- Storytelling
- Research analysis
- Critical theory
- Australian business schools
- Higher education system

Suzanne Ryan is an Associate Professor in the Newcastle Business School at the University of Newcastle, Australia. Her research interests include higher education policy and management, academic labour, business schools and management education. Her primary discipline is organisation theory and her teaching is now primarily in research related courses. She holds various service roles within the University including: Assistant Dean Research Training; member of Academic Senate and President of the University's Branch of the National Tertiary Education Union.

Newcastle Business School, University of Newcastle, Callaghan NSW 2300, Australia

Suzanne.ryan@newcastle.edu.au

Professor James Guthrie is a Professor at Macquarie University, Sydney and Bologna University, Italy. His research and teaching interests include public sector accounting, auditing, accountability and management, social and environmental reporting and auditing, management of knowledge and intellectual capital and the measurement of intangibles. He also consults on public and private sector management, management of knowledge, intellectual capital, budget performance, and annual reporting strategies. He has published widely in both international and national refereed and professional journals and books and has presented his ideas and research findings to over 300 national and international gatherings.

Room 333, Building E4, Macquarie University, NSW, Australia 2109

james.guthrie@mq.edu.au

* The authors would like to thank both Fiona Crawford and Julz Stevens from Macquarie University for their editing and research support.

T HROUGHOUT THE WORLD, UNIVERSITIES HAVE undergone, and are undergoing, significant changes resulting from globalisation, new technology and the adoption of new public management policies by governments and institutions. Major changes include: competition between institutions including global competition for international students; increased student enrolments; higher student–staff ratios; research imperatives and global rankings; more and larger institutions with fewer but larger faculty groupings; and greater accountability to government for proportionately less funding. New public management policies, in particular, have changed universities from social institutions to quasi corporations in which control over academics and their work has increased. The impact of these changes on academics as corporate citizens, engaged and committed to their vocation and institutions, is unclear. On one hand, the scholarly literature depicts a decline in morale, freedom and academic identity, while on the other, official university and government reports demonstrate greater productivity in both research and teaching. Understanding the link between disaffection and compliance is an important, but under-researched, issue that lends itself to new ways of research.

The aim of this paper is to explore the transformational change that took place in Australian graduate schools of business (GSB) in the early 21st century, through the voice and experiences of academics who worked in them. We use storytelling as a medium. The relevance of management[1] research, despite its acknowledged importance, is regularly criticised as failing to impact on 'real life' because of inaccessibility in terms of language, academic conventions and location in scholarly journals (Starkey and Madan, 2001; Pfeffer and Fong, 2002; Bennis and O'Toole, 2005). For critical management scholars, especially those of a Habermasian bent, accessibility of research to the researched is a crucial step in engaging in 'ideal speech' and emancipation. Despite this, critical management scholars are prevented by the same obstacles as their less critical colleagues from reaching the 'subjects' of their research. Understanding the academic environment and its effects on the individual researcher is a step to further understanding the researcher's values and research methods. However, as Rabinow (1986) argues, academic reflexivity rarely extends to the conditions of their own production; our own location within the academy is a taboo.

The results of our research are presented as a story about the hypothetical academic, Bill. Readers are invited to test the veracity of the story and consider the questions it raises about themselves, the role of the researcher and reasons for institutional change. The paper contributes in two ways. First, in the presentation of the research results, providing an innovative and intimate insight into the lifeworld of an academic in a period of significant institutional change. Second, in the novel way in which the research is presented, inviting the reader to identify personally or otherwise with the research and interpret its meaning.

---

1 In this paper business and management are used interchangeably. As in the higher education system, we see a mix of these terms used to describe the faculties and activities under them.

The paper is structured so that it begins by outlining our perspective on critical management research and a role for storytelling. The subsequent section explores the social, political and administrative transformations around the Australian higher education system, followed by an exploration of the method behind the research, including the motivation to employ storytelling to report research results. Next we report the results of our research in the form of a story about Bill. In the final section, we discuss the story's success through an attempt to meet Barone and Eisner's (2006) four criteria for successful storytelling and potential to encourage Habermas' ideal speech. We conclude by inviting the reader to make the final evaluation.

Critical management research and a role for storytelling

In the *Theory of Communicative Action*, Habermas (1984) combines **systems theory** with **theories of social action** to give insight into both the nature of social systems and the experience of the individual or lifeworld. Habermas conceives society as constituted by three 'lifeworlds': the objective (based on instrumental reason), social (based on practical reason) and personal (based on affective reason). With increasing complexity in society, over time the objective lifeworld differentiates itself from the other lifeworlds and is expressed in 'systems' such as the economy. These systems are guided and given meaning by the social lifeworld until they become so complex that 'steering media' are required to guide the systems to align with the lifeworlds (Laughlin, 1987). Increasing differentiation between lifeworld and system is made possible as language develops to articulate the differences; however, because systems are based on instrumental reason, the language decentration that facilitates differentiation eventually allows the system to dominate the lifeworld (Laughlin, 1987; Power and Laughlin, 1992). Possibilities for communication between system and lifeworld decline as the steering media take on a life of their own and employ the mechanisms of 'bureaucratisation' and 'monetarisation' to steer and thus 'colonise' the lifeworld (Burrell, 1994). In response to colonisation, the lifeworld may either defend itself reactively or proactively re-establish its superiority. The latter action is the goal of Habermas' critical theory, emancipation, whereby through communicative action and ideal speech situations, the distinct natures of the system and lifeworld can be understood and rebalanced (Laughlin, 1987).

Emancipation is essentially a form of learning whereby participants may judge whether or not change in social and personal lifeworlds is the result of colonisation by external systems or a form of necessary evolution (for further explanation, see Ryan and Guthrie, 2009). However, emancipation of the researched presents a challenge for critical researchers. While our methods might be distinctly relational in their approach to ensuring interconnectivity between the researcher and the researched (Denzin, 2005) and allow insights into participants' lifeworlds (Alvesson and Karreman, 2000), the goal of emancipation or praxis requires the researcher to return to the field to test the truth claims by generating discussion and consensus among participants (Mingers, 1997), and herein lies the obstacle. For researchers, this final step in the research process is difficult for a range of reasons including elapsed time, pressures to publish, and to do so within conventions and locations not easily accessible to those outside the academic field of study (Bennis and O'Toole, 2005). Indeed, these research pragmatics and pressures may undermine our relationships with research subjects, including our interpretations of their voices (Trainor and Bouchard, 2013) and our ability to be emancipator in the sense of supporting change (Denzin, 2005). With these constraints in mind, we present a means to engage research participants and their like through presenting qualitative research data as a story to facilitate understanding of a process or phenomenon and provoke discussion and possibly change (LeCompte and Schensul, 1999). Because storytelling has the ability to connect minds (Bateson, 2002) and to aid sense-making and expose the taken-for-granted (Weick, 1995), it has the potential to facilitate conditions of ideal speech through reflexivity, Habermas' condition for emancipation.

Form and language in the presentation of research results affects the degree to which participants can identify with the research and with their own stories. Commonly, qualitative research results are interpreted and presented through selections of examples and participant quotations to illustrate themes from the research (Strauss, 1987). This can stifle the voice of the participants by locating their quotations within arguments as well as ignoring the role and voice of the researcher. An alternative presentation is to convert the results into stories where questions of voice and reflexivity become important. Through voice both researcher and research participants can be heard within the text. Traditionally this is achieved through the use of first person and quotations, but 'textual experimentation...can help the researcher to overcome the tendency to write in the distanced and abstracted voice of the disembodied "I"' (Guba and Lincoln, 2005, p. 314). Although such experiments result in 'messy texts', they also 'seek to break the binary between science and literature...and communicate social worlds that have remained private and "non-scientific"' (Guba and Lincoln, 2005, p. 315). Questions of voice are closely linked to questions of reflexivity, the process of critical self-examination by the researcher, 'the conscious experiencing of the self as both inquirer and respondent' (Guba and Lincoln, 2005, p. 314). Textual experimentation, including storytelling, must be 'embedded in the practices of narrativity and reflexivity, without which achieving a voice of (partial) truth is impossible' (Guba and Lincoln, 2005, p. 314).

The use of 'storytelling' as a means of transmitting research results has been recognised as a viable research and teaching tool. Stories in the form of fiction or nonfiction literature have been found to be useful. For instance, Jermier and Domalgalski (2000, p. 62) note that 'literature can convey insights...in a way that is...vivid and memorable, [and] expands understanding of deeper and subtler realms...'. Czarniawska-Joerges and Guillet de Monthoux (1994) advocate the use of fictional literature in management education, recognising that it imparts a phenomenological type of knowledge providing a unique insight. Hansen and Kahnweiler (1993, p. 1393) argue that stories are 'easy to follow, generally entertaining, and are more likely to be remembered'. Pfeffer and Sutton (2006, p. 67) assert 'when used correctly, stories and cases are powerful tools for building management knowledge'.

Storytelling as form of narrative analysis in reporting qualitative data has been adopted from sociology and used by education researchers (for example, Polkinghorne, 1995; Barone, 2001) to 'enhance meanings [and] to broaden and deepen ongoing conversations about education policy and practice' (Barone and Eisner, 2006, p. 102). The success of reporting in this way relies on four consequences arising from the storytelling: illuminating effect; generativity; incisiveness; and generalisability (Barone and Eisner, 2006). **Illuminating effect** refers to the story's ability to reveal what has previously been unnoticed by making 'vivid the subtle but significant' so awareness of what the research is addressing is increased (Barone and Eisner, 2006, p. 102). **Generativity** refers to the story's ability to stimulate new questions. **Incisiveness** refers to the story's ability to go to the heart of the matter and focus the reader's attention on salient issues. And lastly, **generalisability** refers to the story's ability to allow the reader to make connections not previously made by allowing readers to identify with the story and its context. These four criteria fit well within Habermas' notion of communicative action for emancipation through inspiring reflexivity and enabling the conditions for ideal speech, a situation whereby the reader can easily see the collisions between the steering media and personal lifeworlds.

The link between organisation learning and storytelling is well explored within the literature (McAulay and Sims, 2009). Storytelling permits individuals to explore values and beliefs through stories about their own dilemmas and experiences, which in turn benefits individual and group learning (Abma, 2003). For example, significant organisational change creates social drama and 'a period of emotional and interpretative conflict [that is resolved by stakeholders] sharing stories about unfolding events and more implicitly by identifying the plot' (Downing, 1997, p. 27). As critical researchers, we tend to focus on capturing the stories of our subjects, rather than use the art of storytelling to develop individual stories into meta-stories to present our results. Hence what is less explored is the way in which researchers may employ stories to communicate research findings to engage participants in emancipatory conversations. Indeed our aim is to present such a meta-story involving the impacts of system and organisation change on personal and social values.

Context: transformation of the Australian higher education system

University education has become big business over the past two decades with nearly a doubling of higher education students globally including a significant increase in the movement of students across national boundaries. The result is a highly commercialised higher education system in which academics are perceived as little more than commoditised inputs into the process (Parker, 2012).

Public universities are now major drivers of national and local economies as evident in the language of vice chancellors and politicians. Much of the criticism of change in universities is depicted by Parker (2012) as having been driven by a shift in institutional priorities from knowledge accumulation and dissemination to financialisation. Australia provides a clear illustration of the marketisation and globalisation of higher education (see Scott, 1998; Parker, 2011, 2012; Parker and Guthrie, 2013) and within Australian universities business schools make a major contribution to university business models. In 2013, Australian business schools/faculties taught approximately 45% of domestic and international university students, most especially the full fee-paying international and postgraduate students through generally mass delivered, homogeneous and thus highly marketable education.

In an effort to reduce financial outlays and debt and, more recently, to balance budgets after the global financial crisis, governments around the world have made commercialisation, privatisation and corporatisation of the public sector central to their policy initiatives, regardless of political persuasion. Reductions and outsourcing of public services previously delivered directly by government are common, particularly in education, health and welfare (Broadbent and Guthrie, 2008). Under these circumstances, the Australian higher education system has been forced to generate other forms of income, the largest source being the enrolment of full-fee-paying international and postgraduate students. There is now a considerable body of literature that engages with the states of our academic fields and identifies several worrying tendencies (e.g. Burritt *et al.*, 2010; Parker, 2010; Ryan, 2010; Guthrie *et al.*, 2011; Laughlin, 2011; Parker, 2011, 2012; Willmott, 2011).

Since the 1980s, the Australian higher education system has experienced four major waves of change and is undergoing a fifth. The four waves of government-induced policy and funding reform included massification during the 1980s, marketisation in the early 1990s, corporatisation in the late 1990s and early 2000s, and a fourth wave from 2003 to 2007 marked by increased managerialism, greater efficiencies, compliance, quality and research measurements (Ryan *et al.*, 2008). We are now into a new wave of change, marked by an uncapped student system, a powerful quality watchdog, the Tertiary Education Quality Standards Agency, a second generation of research measurement through Excellence in Research Australia (ERA) and a fascination with global rankings, all accompanied by more external and internal measurement, surveillance and control over universities and their academic workforce. Each successive wave has brought with it increased political and economic steering through what Habermas (1984) refers to as the mechanisms of 'bureaucratisation' and 'monetarisation', managerialism and money. Just as the government applies 'bureaucratisation' and 'monetarisation' to steer institutions, so in turn do institutional managers apply the same mechanisms to control their institutions (Marginson and Considine, 2000).

Despite their major contribution to revenue generation, Australian business faculties have relatively poor standing within the university community. Success in commodifying the Australian higher education system and generating revenue has led business schools to be regarded as institutional 'cash cows'. They have not only attracted the largest revenues from fee-paying international and postgraduate coursework students, but minimised costs with the highest staff/ student ratios (Burritt *et al.*, 2010). However, financial success has sometimes been at the cost of academic respect within the university (Ryan and Guthrie, 2009). Business academics are rarely held up as public examples of a university's strength, as the creators of impactful research or contributors to society. Universities have actively encouraged business schools to meet the increasing demand to generate revenue without regard to whether the schools stay within the broader mission of the university (Ryan, 2010). The impacts on the identity and values of business academics in being treated as a business rather than a serious member of the academy have received little if any attention.

Along with managerial tools such as key performance indicators, bonus payments, and contract employment (Guthrie and Parker, 2014; Aronowitz, 2006), the accountability regimes, audit cultures and surveillance mechanisms have the most potential to colonise the academy (Ryan, 2012). These measures reduce 'students to test scores...and teachers to technicians and supervisors in the education assembly line...[it] is fundamentally about the negation of human agency, despite the good intentions of individuals at all levels' (Lipman, cited in Shahjahan, 2011, p. 196). The growth in administration and administrators is noted as indicative of 'the decreasing trust in academics' (Tight, 2010, p. 214), a perceived distrust that in turn undermines shared systems of belief, professional values and our sense of identity as academics (Henkel, 2005). Most under threat is the idea that a university should be a place 'in which nothing is beyond question, not even the current and determined figure of democracy' (Derrida, 2001, p. 253), a place in which the academic's role is no longer to 'understand, interpret, and question' authority but to consolidate it (Giroux, 2006, p. 75). When academic culture is threatened, 'the result can be destructive conflicts between faculties, loss of personal morale and personal alienation' (Dill, 1982, p. 304). Understanding why universities, once sites of resistance, now appear as sites of compliance is complex. Where this issue is addressed, the cause is often attributed to academics engaging reactively in personal alienation rather than collective or public resistance (Ryan, 2012).

Given the nature of their vocation, academics might be expected to reflect on their situation and take action against perceived threats to their environment. However, academic resistance has been minimal at best as individuals prefer to disengage (Anderson, 2008; Parker and Jary, 1995; Willmott, 1995). Even the professoriate, which may have been expected to uphold academic values and oppose such instrumentalisation of the academy, has failed to do so, preferring either to shun the inconvenience and risk of engaging in resistance (Barney, 2010) or, as itself a victim of bureaucratisation and monetarisation processes, finding its ability to lead has been undermined (Macfarlane, 2011). Willmott (1995, p. 1023) explains the general preference to withdraw being based on academics being 'ill equipped to interpret the significance of change'. Anderson's (2008) study of resistance among Australian academics finds individual withdrawal a form of resistance, indeed the most common form used to protect professional values and identity. Respondents in Anderson's research were angered by managerial discourse and practices but generally refused to engage with them, preferring to complain to trusted colleagues or minimise their compliance effort. This form of passive individual resistance is framed by an understanding of academic culture and so attempts 'to limit the process of colonisation implicit in the managerial project' (Anderson, 2008, p. 267).

Current imperatives to commodify teaching, to measure and commercialise research and to account continually for what academics do had no role in the traditional academic experience and value set but are now a part of their daily discourse. Over time and within the change process, new values are not clearly articulated, so that change occurs through a process of sedimentation, in which 'new ideals are layered on top of existing ones', some of which are ultimately absorbed, replacing earlier values, and some of which are rejected (Bleiklie, 2005, p. 200). It is during the process of sedimentation or change that values are either colonised or evolved. Understanding the nature and extent of colonisation and evolution of academic lifeworld values was the aim of the original research for this paper. The point of our 'story' is to better equip academics in understanding the significance of their changing environments and ultimately in making judgements on how change has affected them personally.

Method

Sample

The story is based on the results of a broader longitudinal research project into the tensions between academic values and the corporatisation of higher education using Australian graduate schools of business as a case study. The data are from interviews with academics in three autonomous graduate schools in 2002 and 2008. Participants are viewed as the one sample from one hypothetical graduate school of business, referred to as 'the School' or the 'AGSB' and their initial selection reflected the disciplines, age, academic ranking and gender composition of the School population. In 2002, 21 academics were interviewed representing 25% of the full-time academic population of the three schools. Of the original 21 academics, 18 were re-interviewed in 2008. Only five remained in the same school in 2008 although all had continued either working or teaching in business schools, including three who had resigned or retired from academe. A story based on the 2002 round of interviews was sent back to participants for verification and then used again as a segue into the 2008 follow-up interviews.

Analysis

Interviews ranging from 60 minutes to four hours were held with the participants. The transcripts were analysed in the conventional way of coding and theming based on a priori and emergent codes. However, we were not interested in adopting a grounded theory approach (Parker, 2010) and developing an explanatory model, as this would have been contrary to our Habermasian philosophy. In the process of writing up the data from the 2002 round of interviews, it became obvious how similar were the individual stories including the content, codes and even the metaphors. This realisation led to the idea of combining the transcripts into a single 'story' to send to participants as a means of verifying the overall research results. At the time, it seemed like a natural progression, but after the 2008 interviews, developing a 'story' required greater skill and justification. Hence, the need to further investigate 'storytelling' as a technique arose and led to an understanding of discourse analyses, their various methods and objectives.

In this regard, Alvesson and Karreman (2000, p. 1126) distinguish between discourse analysis with a focus on the text and discourse analysis as the study 'of social reality as discursively constructed' to form and articulate ideas of a particular period. This latter form of analysis, referred to by Alvesson and Karreman as 'Discourse, with a capital D' or *long-range* analysis, goes beyond the text to consider social context and subjects—'to just hear the story' (p. 1145). It summarises, synthesises and blends individual transcripts to 'identify overarching themes operating in specific situations' (p. 1134). In doing so individual differences and local variations are inevitably glossed over in order to capture the meta-story. Additionally, an order to the meta-analysis is imposed by the authors whereby the more subtle identity work found in *close-range* discourse analysis may be lost. In acknowledging these limitations, we concur with Alvesson and Karreman that 'rigor should sometimes be downplayed for the benefit of social relevance' (p. 1134). In creating our story, we chose to refract rather than mirror the past and, in doing so, to create a story that would engage and provoke by making connections among past, present and future events (Riessman, 2003). However, unlike some forms of narrative work that involve the creation of stories involving causality and plot, we were not concerned with developing a 'plot', preferring instead to allow readers to make their own judgements as to the type of story (Bunia, 2010).

In creating our story, we adopted a *long-range* approach and conflated the interview transcripts around a single individual, the hypothetical academic, Bill, to represent the 'voice' of all the GSB academics in our study. We constructed Bill's gender, rank and age based on the median profile of the participants in 2008: for example, two-thirds of the participants were male and the median age was 51. In 2002, participant responses in the interview transcripts were similar with little variation among the 21 academics, so generating a story for this period was not difficult. In addition to the similarity in responses, the social environments of the three graduate schools of business were also alike and quite distinct from other academic departments and schools. However, by

2008, the environments had changed and all but 5 of the 18 interviewed had left their GSB and moved on to work in other schools, universities, or in positions outside universities. Although this presented a challenge to using the 'one voice' to represent the whole group, participants' reflections on changes in the intervening years reflected similar themes. Hence we continued with the 'one voice' of Bill to capture the common themes and use his references to colleagues to capture variations.

As long time management academics, this story was close to our hearts and own experiences. Although based on data from interviews and monitoring of changes in the Australian higher education system, we take full responsibility for the form and language of the story. Studying our own colleagues overcame difficulties associated with being perceived as a 'voyeur' or 'informant' or of having only a 'partial picture' of the subject because the researcher is of a different background (Lapsely, 2004). On the other hand, being an 'insider' can lead to its own biases and assumptions that require engagement in 'self-critical reflexivity' (McSweeny, 2004). Compared to our initial work in coding, theme development and identification of relevant quotations, writing the story forced us to be more self-reflexive and questioning of the texts. Additionally, by using Barone and Eisner's (2006) criteria for guiding and evaluating storytelling, we were obliged to consider issues of subjectivity and accessibility.

Bill's story

The story opens with Bill living a busy but contented life within a strong collegial graduate school, the success of which is a direct result of earlier changes to the Australian higher education system. He is the epitome of the corporate citizen. However, over a period of six years, Bill becomes increasingly unhappy and detached as his institution's managerialism affects his everyday life and identity. His corporate citizenship appears to be undermined by changes in his environment. In a short period the small, interdisciplinary, stand-alone GSB have almost disappeared from Australia (reduced from about 15 in the year 2000 to only 1 in 2014) and have been swallowed up in amalgamations into super-business faculties based on strict disciplines and offering programmes to undergraduates and postgraduates from both domestic and international student 'markets'. The story is set against changes in the Australian higher education system as discussed above. While the waves of marketisation and corporatisation allowed Bill to live an exciting academic life and become the almost perfect corporate citizen, the fourth wave of change, managerialism, signalled the end of the excitement and presented a challenge to his academic freedom, values and identity. Ultimately the story and its interpretation pose the question as to whether Bill's values and identity were colonised or evolved by changes to the university system.

Five Years in the Life of Bill: an average academic in an Australian graduate school of business

I first met Bill in 2002 in his office at the Australian Graduate School of Business (AGSB). The school buildings and surroundings were quite palatial compared to other parts of the university but Bill's office reflected that of a typical academic with books and papers strewn everywhere. He was 45 at the time and had worked at the AGSB for seven years as a Senior Lecturer. Before this, Bill had worked in three other business schools totalling 16 years as an academic. He moved into an academic career from a position in private industry where he studied for his MBA part-time. His study became more exciting than his work so that, on completing his MBA, he enrolled in a PhD and began part-time teaching. This was the turning point for Bill. He so enjoyed teaching and what he saw to be the life of his full-time colleagues that when the opportunity arose, he surrendered his job in industry to become an academic. Although the move to academe involved a substantial reduction in salary, Bill considered the freedom of being in control of his own work and time with thought-provoking colleagues was sufficient compensation. He had resented the control and command culture of working in a large private sector organisation.

After 16 years as an academic, Bill remained satisfied with his work, especially the freedom over what he teaches and researches and the time in which he does it. Additionally, he enjoyed the school environment, describing it as hard working, friendly and collegial, collegial in terms of respect for colleagues rather than governance. His colleagues were highly motivated and his classes stimulating. One small disappointment for Bill was that, although the school and its flagship programme, the MBA, were multidisciplinary, the achievement of true interdisciplinarity was unnecessarily restricted by a disciplinary focus from research and publication requirements. Students were a special pleasure to Bill because of their maturity and motivation; he viewed them as an important source of his own learning. However, the fact that they paid high fees sometimes encouraged them to behave like customers, not a behaviour with which he felt comfortable. Despite equally valuing research and teaching, Bill admitted that teaching took precedence because of the urgency of deadlines and the expectations of the students. Being a good teacher is important to both Bill and the AGSB.

Bill's first loyalty was to the school and his colleagues, although he was ambiguous about his feelings for the position of dean and critical of the central university administration. Several deans had passed through the school since Bill joined. According to Bill, deans come and go, but the culture and collegiality of AGSB academics are stronger than a single dean. A good dean is a valuable asset to the school but a bad dean causes unnecessary distractions and politics. The autonomous governance of the AGSB was important to Bill, regardless of the deans' dispositions. Central university administrators threatened the school's autonomy because they were uncomfortable with its difference and wanted a greater percentage of its revenue. Over the years Bill noticed that the number of administrators had increased while support to academics had decreased, leading to greater pressure in every aspect of work. Inappropriate bureaucratic administrative processes were a particular source of frustration emanating from the central university administration but not the school's administrative staff, whom Bill considered part of the school 'team'. Bill admitted that neither he nor his colleagues took university processes very seriously, complying with them in terms of the letter rather than the spirit of the law.

When I first interviewed Bill, it had taken a while to make an appointment because Bill's schedule included a teaching trip to Hong Kong for ten days followed by teaching an intensive development course for executives at a retreat outside the city. Most of his teaching was carried out in intensive blocks in the evenings and at weekends. When I asked Bill about his lifestyle and when he found time for research and family, Bill admitted it was sometimes quite stressful, but he was well compensated for the additional work. Teaching overseas and in intensive blocks provided good opportunities to write up his research while executive education and consulting kept him up to date with the latest issues and practice, which in turn informed his teaching. Overseas teaching was also a time to socialise with colleagues teaching at the same time. Although he enjoyed the experience of being in Asia for his own education, the students were weaker than the local students and it did take its toll on health and family life. The initial attraction of travel and additional remuneration wore off after a few visits. Overall, Bill much preferred the lifestyle of an AGSB academic to being in a large undergraduate business school where he thought the culture was weaker and more negative, the resources fewer and with less remuneration or opportunities for additional earnings. On the issue of earnings, Bill was adamant that any additional remuneration was only commensurate with his additional effort compared with non-AGSB academics.

After over two hours of talking with Bill, I asked my last question: what his ideal life would involve. He thought for a while before answering and then responded saying he was really quite content with his work and life at the AGSB but at the edges it could be improved if there were more time for research and less managerialism and administrative interference. As I left the AGSB, I reflected on how different Bill's story was from the results of large aggregate surveys of Australian academic life at the time. While Bill appeared to be enjoying his academic life, his colleagues elsewhere were indicating their greatest job dissatisfaction since such surveys began. Over a decade of government policies aimed at deregulating higher education had created stress and frustration among most academics. However, Bill and his colleagues appeared to have benefited from the same policies that allowed fee-paying international and postgraduate students into the system. As a result, the AGSB was better resourced than other academic units and Bill enjoyed the entrepreneurial spirit within the school.

I met Bill several times at conferences over the next few years where we spoke briefly, exchanging news and a few pleasantries. In 2008, it was time to formally meet again to follow-up on the first interview. I sent Bill a copy of the story based on a consolidation of the 2002 transcripts as well as his own transcript with a request that we meet to discuss what had changed in the intervening period. This time it was much easier to find a time to meet. Bill had reduced his additional teaching and ceased to consult or teach on executive programmes in order to spend more time on research and publications. As a result of increased research output, he had risen from Senior Lecturer to an Associate Professor. His office was much the same; however, his tone was different and it became evident that this was not because of the promotion. Bill was now over 50 and concerned with how he would spend his final decade or so of work. What had happened both to Bill and the AGSB over the past years had given him cause to look elsewhere for work. He now spent several hours a week looking for, or thinking about, other jobs, stirred by his disillusionment and discomfort with the direction and values of those controlling the AGSB.

Among the several reasons Bill gave for his current attitude, are the following. He complained that work pressure has increased, especially pressure to publish and apply for grants, but the satisfaction from work has decreased. Most of his colleagues have left and the school culture has changed from one of stimulation to one of control. Among those colleagues who remain, including Bill himself, most of their time is spent working from home to avoid what they perceive as a negative environment. The battle to retain AGSB autonomy was lost and the school was soon to be merged into the large undergraduate faculty based on the argument that a greater critical mass of discipline-based researchers was needed to meet national research assessment requirements. The once intermittent annoying administrative intrusions on his work had become relentless. There was no choice but to take them seriously as policies and processes had come to represent what was most important to the university. In order to increase fee revenue, student eligibility requirements had been lowered and Bill no longer enjoyed teaching as he did before. He complained that the younger full-time students were less motivated with poorer language skills, more demanding and less intellectually challenging. The classroom was not the 'bear pit of ideas' that it once was. Unlike before, Bill looked forward to teaching offshore not only because it allowed him a break from the stress of work, but also he now found the students relatively better than those onshore.

Bill still remained in contact with his colleagues who left the AGSB. While most left to find employment in other business schools, some retired or left academic life to become consultants. Regardless of what they have done, they tell Bill that their lives are less pressured but not quite as satisfying nor exciting as in the heyday of the AGSB. Those colleagues who left academic employment continue to teach casually because they enjoy it but do not regret having left. A few of Bill's colleagues accepted managerial positions within universities where they have gained a broader view of the university system. For some, this experience has led them to strive to protect their academic staff from bureaucratic excesses while for a minority of others who embraced the management regime, they look back and see flaws in their former AGSB life and colleagues, especially their own and their former colleagues' lack of empathy for senior executives.

On the subject of academic managers, Bill no longer believes that the AGSB culture is stronger than the deans that pass through it. In recent years there has been a high turnover of deans, some on the side of the central university management and trying to bring the AGSB under control while others fought against central control. Either way, the university management won out, with or without the help of the deans. The AGSB culture was forced to change as so many of its academics abandoned ship, including the deans who had fought to maintain its autonomy. Collegiality and entrepreneurialism no longer came to mind when Bill described the new culture, for which he chose words like alienated, disengaged and transactional. His new colleagues have *not experienced the possibilities of the past and, much to Bill's frustration, appear to accept things as they are. Although still valuing the freedom over what and how he teaches and researches and uses his time, Bill has lost his feeling of ownership and belonging toward the AGSB, withdrawing into his own work and world. The obsession with making money and measuring publications has undermined his understanding of 'quality' in teaching and research and intensified his cynicism of official versions of 'quality'.*

Bill's lifestyle continues to be that of an itinerant, working non-traditional hours, in multiple locations but he is tiring of it, feeling there is no longer sufficient reward, intrinsic or extrinsic, for working to such a schedule. The departure of colleagues, along with changes to governance structures, altered the school culture to the point where Bill feels like a factory employee rather than an academic colleague. The passion for his school has turned to indifference. Despite his continual search for a new position outside the AGSB, Bill is held back from ever following through. In the back of his mind ring the comments of colleagues who left for other universities that it's not very different elsewhere, it's just that the pain of change came earlier in other places so it is easier to get on with life. 'Getting on with life' seems to be the message from the latest aggregate survey of academics in Australia. Although distrust of university management remains high throughout the sector, the survey reports improved job satisfaction and institutional commitment.

I wish Bill luck with whatever he decides to do and leave his office puzzled about what has really happened to him. Obviously his world has changed and it is not a change that sits comfortably with him. But is he just grieving over a glorified past or fighting passively to save what he believes is important? Would acceptance of the new order involve a change in his fundamental values or simply a reorientation of his behaviour to adjust to what others have deemed a necessary change in the system? Is his obvious regret about the change a symptom of resistance to the change or resignation?

Discussion

Our discussion of the story, the results of our research, is built around Barone and Eisner's (2006) four criteria for guiding and evaluating storytelling: illuminating effect; generativity; incisiveness; and generalisability. Specifically, we tried to meet each of the four criteria and so encourage discussion of academic life in the following ways.

First, in terms of **illuminating effect** or the story's ability to reveal what has previously been unnoticed or taken for granted, we chose to focus on the one character, Bill, an amalgam of the academic participants with additional references to his colleagues to indicate variations from Bill's experience. We employed the conflated voice to force focus on the impact of change on the individual without the distraction of other voices. Such individual focus increases understanding of personal lifeworld values and beliefs and changes in the objective lifeworld. For example, we see Bill professing a continuous valuing of his academic freedom over the period while we also read of his unhappiness and obvious compliance with central management imperatives to behave in other ways. The conflict between the belief in his freedom (personal lifeworld) and the external control of his behaviour (by steering media) results in Bill's withdrawal, alienation and indifference and illuminates issues that might otherwise be overlooked in traditional reporting of results. In communicating a private world of subtle contradictions and comparisons, albeit in a 'nonscientific' way, the story is able to reveal new insights and generate new questions (Guba and Lincoln, 2005).

The second criterion for success in storytelling, **generativity**, relates to the story's ability to stimulate new questions. Our central question, which we overtly raise at the end of the story, refers to whether Bill's lifeworld was colonised or in a process of positive evolution. However, in writing up the story, other questions arose about Bill and other actors, questions such as: why was it taking Bill so long to 'move on' compared to colleagues who had left? Does 'sedimentation' or evolution take longer if you remain in the same location (Bleiklie, 2005)? Was Bill's situation one of evolutionary transition or passive resistance (Ryan, 2012)? Why does Bill appear to ignore his own agency in not resisting change (Anderson, 2008)? Were the colleagues and deans who accepted the new management regimes more quickly colonised or evolved and why? Were the values of new colleagues really different from Bill's or was it simply that their experiences differed from his? How long will Bill be able to withstand the contradictions between his beliefs and his behaviour? And the related question of what would happen to Bill, would he 'move on' by leaving, evolving, or actively resisting? Ultimately, these and other new questions will be for the reader to consider. The important point is that the reader is stimulated to ask questions of the story and consider their relevance to the reader's life.

To address the third criterion, **incisiveness**, in order to get to the heart of the matter and focus on the important issues, we wrote the story so that external changes in system and university were told through Bill's experiences and the impacts of change largely explained through his emotive reactions (affective reason) to, rather than evaluations (instrumental reason) of, change in the higher education systems (objective lifeworld). For example, the research priority, the new students and colleagues and greater administrative control are evidence of system change, while the loss of ownership, feelings of alienation and frustration are the personal reactions. The distinction between emotion and evaluation is important as it is the former that provides greater insight into the personal lifeworld. At certain points in the story we editorialise and introduce information on sector wide surveys as a device to provide background information and comparison that would raise questions about differences between Bill and other academics outside graduate business schools. In a more subtle way, the use of storytelling is also a means of demonstrating the power of this method compared to aggregate surveys. Similar contradiction may exist among survey respondents but the reporting of surveys does not allow such subtleties to emerge. The use of a single conflated voice aids in making the story more incisive. Although it may appear to make the story one-sided, it forces the reader to concentrate on system impacts on the individual without the diversion of other voices. It forces the reader to concentrate on the collisions between personal lifeworld and steering media.

Finally, in terms of the fourth criterion, **generalisability**, or the story's ability to allow the reader to identify with the story and its context, this must be left for the reader to judge. 'Critical research tries to engage in the power dynamics of truth in organisations without setting itself up as the final arbitrator of truth claims' (Alvesson and Deetz, 2000, p. 47). We therefore invite the reader to judge the degree to which she or he identifies with the story and to consider, among other questions, the broader issue of whether Bill was colonised by changes in the Australian higher education system or was in the process of evolution and to what degree. Identification with Bill's story is central to provoking reflexivity about one's own situation and values. It further provides a platform for discussion with colleagues, a more informed 'corridor talk' (Rabinow, 1986).

In relation to this central question, *was Bill colonised?*, if we accept the advice of Broadbent *et al.* (1991) that evaluation of change should be made from the perspective of active organisational participants in specific institutions at particular points in time, then it may be impossible to ever provide a general answer to the question as both institutions and individuals change with time. There is also the possibility for opposing institutional logics to co-exist within the same organisation (Reay and Hinings, 2009). In the context of the 'sacred and secular divide' whereby some organisational values are more important (sacred) than others (secular), then any intrusion by the secular into the sacred is always resisted but secular concerns are generally of lesser importance and if they are not perceived to threaten the sacred, then they are not resisted (Laughlin, 2007). If this reasoning is applied to universities, then it may explain why managerialism (the secular) has not been strongly resisted. However, in Habermasian terms of competing dualisms, the danger is always that the secular (steering media) will potentially infiltrate the sacred (lifeworld) by stealth unless we are made aware through communicative action of what is occurring.

Although a plot was not used in the development of our story (Bunia, 2010), with hindsight, the story seems to us to be one of loss, or at least a story in need of a final instalment to resolve Bill's dilemma and ours. An obvious avenue of further research is to follow up the original research participants for part three. As far as we know, at least 16 of the original 21 remain as academics, either full-time or retired but continuing to carry out research or casual teaching. Aside from the specific research emerging from this paper, we would urge researchers to follow our lead and experiment with the presentation of results in story form based on Alvesson and Karreman's (2000) 'Discourse, with a capital D', analysis. Answers and explanations to questions such as ours perhaps only come from hindsight; however, the use of storytelling to translate research results into overarching themes and meta-stories at specific times in history provides an exceptionally rich source of information and provocation for future research (Alvesson and Karreman, 2000). Furthermore engaging in creative forms of written communication is 'a counter to the dead weight of uncreative compliance with customary practice' (Hey, 2001). Storytelling is a means of both stimulating our own reflexivity and advancing ideal speech situations in order that we better understand the connections between systems and lifeworlds and are able to rebalance or resist them as required for emancipation.

References

Abma, T. A. (2003), 'Learning by telling: Storytelling workshops as an organizational learning intervention', *Management Learning*, Vol. 34, No. 2, pp. 221-40.

Alvesson, M. and Deetz, S. (2000) *Doing Critical Management Research*, Sage, London.

Alvesson, M. and Karreman, D. (2000), 'Varieties of discourse: On the study of organisations through discourse analysis', *Human Relations*, Vol. 53, No 9, pp. 1125-1149.

Anderson, G. (2008), 'Mapping academic resistance in the managerial university', *Organization*, Vol. 15, No. 2, pp. 251-270.

Aronowitz, S. (2006), 'Should academic unions get involved in governance', *Liberal Education*, Vol. 92, No. 4, pp. 22-27.

Barney, D. (2010) 'Miserable priests and ordinary cowards: On being a professor', *Journal of Cultural Studies*, Vols 23-24 (Fall), pp. 381-387.

Barone, T. (2001), 'Science, art and the predispositions of educational researchers', *Educational Researcher*, Vol. 30, No 7, pp. 24-28.

Barone, T. and Eisner, E. (2006), 'Arts-based educational research', in J. L. Green, G. Camilli and P. B. Elmore (eds) *Handbook of Complementary Methods in Education Research*, American Educational Research Association, Lawrence Erlbaum Associates Inc, pp. 95-110.

Bateson, G. (2002) *Mind and Nature: A Necessary Unity*, Hampton Press, Creskill, NJ.

Bennis, W. G. and O'Toole, J. (2005), 'How business schools lost their way', *Harvard Business Review*, May, pp. 96-104.

Bleiklie, I. (2005), 'Academic leadership and emerging knowledge regimes', in I. Bleiklie and M. Henkel (eds.), *Governing Knowledge: A Study of Continuity and Change in Higher Education—A Festchrift in Honour of Maurice Kogan*, Springer, The Netherlands, pp. 189-212.

Broadbent, J. and Guthrie, J. (2008) 'Public sector to public services: 20 years of "alternative" accounting research', *Accounting, Auditing and Accountability Journal*, Vol. 21, No. 2, pp. 129-169.

Broadbent, J., Laughlin, R. and Read, S. (1991), 'Recent financial and administrative changes in the NHS: A critical theory analysis', *Critical Perspectives in Accounting*, Vol. 2, No. 1, pp. 1-29.

Bunia, R. (2010), 'Diegesis and representation: Beyond the fictional world, on the margins of story and narrative', *Poetics Today*, Vol. 31, No. 4, pp. 679-720.

Burrell, G. (1994) 'Modernism, postmodernism and organizational analysis 4: The contribution of Jurgen Habemas', *Organizational Studies*, Vol. 15, No. 1, pp. 1-45.

Burritt, R., Evans, E. and Guthrie, J. (eds) (2010), 'Challenges for accounting education at a crossroad in 2010', *Academic Leadership Series*, Vol. 1, pp. 9-15.

Czarniawska-Joerges, B. and Guillet de Monthoux, P. (eds) (1994), *Good Novels, Better Management: Reading Organizational Realities in Fiction*, Routledge, London.

Denzin, N. K. (2005), 'Emancipatory discourses and the ethics and politics of interpretation', *The Sage Handbook of Qualitative Research*, Vol. 3, pp. 933-958.

Derrida, J. (2001), 'The future of the profession or the unconditional university', in L. Simmons and H. Worth (eds) *Derrida Down Under*, Dunmarra Press, Auckland, NZ.

Dill, D. (1982), 'The management of academic culture: Notes on the management of meaning and social integration', *Higher Education*, Vol. 11, No. 3, pp. 303-320.

Downing, S. J. (1997), 'Learning the plot: Emotional momentum in search of dramatic logic, *Management Learning*, Vol. 28, No. 1, pp. 27-44.

Giroux, H. A. (2006), 'Higher education under siege: Implications for public intellectuals', *Thought and Action*, Fall, pp. 63-78.

Guba, E. G. and Lincoln, Y. S. (2005), 'Paradigmatic controversies, contradictions, and emerging influences', in N. K. Denzin and Y. S. Lincoln (eds), *The Sage Handbook of Qualitative Research* (3rd edn), Sage, Thousand Oaks, CA, pp. 191-215.

Guthrie, J. and Parker, L. (2014), 'The global accounting academic: What counts', *Accounting, Auditing and Accountability Journal*, Vol. 27, No. 1.

Guthrie, J., Burritt, R. and Evans, E. (2011), 'The relationship between academic accounting research and professional practice', *Academic Leadership Series*, Vol. 2, pp. 9-20.

Habermas, J. (1984), *The Theory of Communicative Action, Volume One, Reason and the Rationalisation of Society*, Beacon Press, Boston.

Hansen, C. D. and Kahnweiler, W. M. (1993), 'Storytelling: An instrument for understanding the dynamics of corporate relationships', *Human Relations*, Vol. 46, No. 12, pp. 1391–1400.

Henkel, M. (2005), 'Academic identity and autonomy in a changing policy environment', *Higher Education*, Vol. 49, Nos 1–2, pp. 155-176.

Hey, V. (2001) 'The construction of academic time:sub/contracting academic labour in research', *Journal of Education Policy*, Vol. 16, No. 1, pp. 67-84.

Jermier, J. M. and Domalgalski, T. (2000), 'Storytelling and organizational studies: A critique of "Learning about work from Joe Cool"', *Journal of Management Inquiry*, Vol. 9, pp. 62–64.

Lapsley, I. (2004), 'Making sense of interaction in an investigation of organisational practices and processes', in C. Humphrey and B. Lee (eds.), *The Real Life Guide to Accounting Research: A Behind-the Scenes View of using Qualitative Research Methods*, Elsevier, Oxford, pp. 75-190.

Laughlin, R. C. (1987) 'Accounting systems in organisational contexts: A case for critical theory', *Accounting, Organizations and Society*, Vol. 12, No. 5, pp. 479-502.

Laughlin, R. (2007), 'Critical reflections on research approaches, accounting regulation and the regulation of accounting', *The British Accounting Review*, Vol. 39, No. 4, pp. 271-289.

Laughlin, R. (2011), 'Accounting research, policy and practice: World together or worlds apart?', *Academic Leadership Series*, Vol. 2, pp. 21-30.

LeCompte, M.D. and Schensul, J.J. (1999), *Designing and Conducting Ethnographic Research*, AltaMira, Walnut Creek, CA.

McAulay, L. and Sims, D. (2009), 'Management learning as a learning process: An invitation', *Management Learning*, Vol. 26, No. 1, pp. 5-20.

Macfarlane, B. (2011), 'Professors as intellectual leaders: Formation, identity and role', *Studies in Higher Education*, Vol. 36, No. 1, pp. 57-73.

McSweeny, B. (2004), 'Critical independence', in C. Humphrey and B. Lee (eds.), *The Real Life Guide to Accounting Research: A Behind-the Scenes View of using Qualitative Research Methods*, Elsevier, Oxford, pp. 207-226.

Marginson, S. and Considine, M. (2000), *The Enterprise University: Power, Governance and Reinvention in Australia*, Cambridge University Press, Cambridge.

Mingers, J. (1997), 'Multiparadigm multimethodology' in J. Mingers and A. Gill (eds.), *Multimethodology: The Theory and Practice of Combining Management Science Methodologies*, John Wiley, pp. 1-19.

Parker, L. (2010), 'Introducing the commercialised university environment: Preliminary reflections on the trajectory of change', *Academic Leadership Series*, Vol. 1, pp. 16-21.

Parker, L. (2011), 'University corporatisation: Driving redefinition', *Critical Perspectives on Accounting*, Vol. 22, No. 4, pp. 434-450.

Parker, L. (2012), 'From privatised to hybrid corporatised higher education: A global financial management discourse', *Financial Accountability and Management*, Vol. 28, No. 3, pp. 1-22.

Parker, L. and Guthrie J. (2013), 'Accounting scholars and journals rating and benchmarking: Risking academic research quality', *Accounting, Auditing and Accountability Journal*, Vol. 26, No. 1, pp. 4–15.

Parker, M. and Jary, D. (1995), 'The McUniversity: Organisation, management and academic subjectivity', *Organization*, Vol. 2, No. 2, pp. 319-338.

Pfeffer, J. and Fong, C. (2002) The end of business schools? Less success than meets the eye, *Academy of Management Learning and Education*, Vol. 1, No. 1, 78-95.

Pfeffer, J. and Sutton, R. (2006), 'Evidence-based management', *Harvard Business Review*, Vol. 84, No. 1, pp. 62–74.

Polkinghorne, D. E. (1995), 'Narrative configuration in qualitative analysis', *International Journal of Qualitative Studies in Education*, Vol. 8, No. 1, pp. 5-23.

Power, M. and Laughlin, R. (1992), 'Habermas, law and accounting', *Accounting, Organisations and Society*, Vol. 21, No. 2, pp. 441- 465.

Rabinow, P. (1986) 'Representations are social facts: Modernity and postmodernity in anthropology', in J. Cliford and G Marcus (eds) *Writing Culture: The Poetics and Politics of Ethnography*, Harvard University Press, Cambridge, MA.

Reay, T. and Hinings, C.R. (2009), 'Managing the rivalry of competing institutional logics', *Organizational Studies*, Vol. 30, No. 6, pp. 629-52.

Riessman, C. K. (2003), 'Narrative analysis' in M.S. Lewis-Beck, A. Bryman and T. Futing Liao (eds.), *The Sage Encyclopedia of Social Science Research Methods*, 3 Vols. Sage, pp. 1-17.

Ryan, S. (2010), 'Business and accounting education: Do they have a future in the university?' *Academic Leadership Series*, Vol. 1, pp. 9-15.

Ryan, S. (2012), 'Academic zombies: A failure of resistance or a means of survival?', *Australian Universities Review*, Vol. 54, No. 2, pp. 3-11.

Ryan, S. and Guthrie, J. (2009), 'Evaluating change in the Australian Higher Education System: A critical theory perspective', *ANZAM 09 Conference*, Melbourne, 2–5 December.

Ryan, S., Guthrie, J. and Neumann, R. (2008), 'The case of Australian Higher Education: Performance, markets and government control', in C. Mazza, P. Quattrone and A. Riccaboni (eds.), *European Universities in Transition: Issues, Models and Cases*, Edward Elgar, London, pp. 171-187.

Scott P. (1998), 'Massification, internationalisation and globalisation', in P. Scott (ed.), *The Globalisation of Higher Education*, Society for Research into Higher Education and Open University Press, Buckingham.

Shahjahan, R.A. (2011), 'Decolonising the evidence-based education and policy movement: Revealing the colonial vestiges in education policy, research and neoliberal reform', *Journal of Education Policy*, Vol. 26, No. 2, pp. 181-206.

Starkey, K. and Madan, P. (2001) 'Bridging the relevance gap: Aligning stakeholders in the future of management research', *British Journal of Management*, Vol. 12, Special Issue, S3-S26.

Strauss, A. (1987), *Qualitative Analysis for Social Scientists*, Cambridge University Press, New York.

Tight, M. (2010), 'Are academic workloads increasing? The post-war survey evidence in the UK', *Higher Education Quarterly*, Vol. 64, No. 2, pp. 200-215.

Trainor, A. and Bouchard, K. A. (2013), 'Exploring and developing reciprocity in research design', *International Journal of Qualitative Studies in Education*, Vol. 26, No. 8, pp. 986-1003.

Weick, K (1995) *Sensemaking in Organisations*, Sage, USA.

Willmott, H. (1995), 'Managing the academics: Commodification and control in the development of university education in the UK', *Human Relations*, Vol. 48, No. 9, pp. 993-1027.

Willmott, H. (2011), 'Journal list fetishism and the perversion of scholarship: Reactivity and the ABS list', *Organization*, Vol. 18, No. 4, pp. 429-442.

Mopping up Institutional Racism

Activism on a Napkin

Heather Came
Auckland University of Technology, New Zealand

Maria Humphries
Waikato University, New Zealand

Racism is an anathema to a just society. Overt expressions of personal racism are frowned upon in 'nice' homes, at progressive boardroom tables, in liberal churches, in the critical classrooms of universities, and in the many places privileged people meet. Institutional(ised) racism, however, has yet to attract such widespread recognition and a similar public discouragement. We are aware of, and engaged with, many expressions of such racism in Aotearoa, a country renamed as New Zealand by the colonisers. In this paper we focus on how institutional racism manifests within public health policies and funding practices in this country distilled into a handy napkin-sized conversation starter. We see the moral integrity of managers as a necessary conduit to institutional and therefore social transformation. We urge their responsible actions in their corporate citizenship in seeking innovations that wipe out institutional(ised) racism and embed practices that are just for all.

- Institutional racism
- Activist scholarship
- Public sector
- Health policy and funding
- Critical management education

Heather Came is a seventh generation Pākehā New Zealander and a first generation activist who has been working in health promotion/public health and with Te Tiriti o Waitangi for 20 years. She currently teaches at AUT University, is an active member of Tamaki Tiriti Workers and is involved in a national campaign to end institutional racism within the public health sector.

Department of Public Health, Auckland University of Technology, Private Bag 92006, Auckland 1142, New Zealand

Heather.came@aut.ac.nz

Maria Humphries came to New Zealand with her migrant parents in 1960. The existence of Te Tiriti o Waitangi and its implications for a just New Zealand was drawn to her attention in the late 1980s by a group of local activists who sought to draw wider acknowledgement and respect among Pākehā to this document. How integrity of relationships, including Treaty relationships might be included in the education of managers is part of her professional concern. Maria is currently an Associate Professor at Waikato Management School teaching critical management studies.

Waikato Management School, Waikato University, Private Bag 3015, University of Waikato, Hamilton 3240, New Zealand

Mariah@waikato.ac.nz

Question: 'What are you researching?'

Answer: 'Institutional racism within public health policymaking and funding practices in Aotearoa[1] that undermine the wellbeing of Māori[2] in this land. We are interested in how activist research might contribute to its transformation...'

Interruption: 'How interesting...'

EYES AROUND THE TABLE GLAZE over. The conversation moves to a different topic. This polite disengagement from a deep conversation about something as uncomfortable as institutional(ised) racism will not be unique to our experience. Researchers in any field that challenges the comfort zones of those with social privilege will recognise this disengagement in polite company. Our commitment to staying in the conversation is an integral and necessary part of being anti-racism researchers. Raising the topic at the tables of the privileged may seem like a small action. It is, however, part of a broader activist agenda that seeks to expand a small chink in the delusions of those who want to believe that we are living in and contributing to a just world. Are we, the good among the privileged, living a lie? Now that really is a scary dinner-time topic! Our passion to remain engaged in conversations about institutional(ised) racism and its necessary transformation has drawn us into research that directly challenges such racism, and into writing about such racism as a choice of focus. This choice of focus is itself an activist choice.

Activist scholarship is about recognising competing knowledge claims and unravelling the complex political matters that give rise to the unjust outcomes of unequal influence on the discourses through which we organise our humanity. Such work entails cracking codes of silence and exposing the lies and delusions of the master narrative, that beguiling cloak of reason that pervades so much common sense, infuses our institutional protocols, and directs our manners. It involves ongoing dialogue and accountability between scholars and activist communities. However commitments to action go beyond dialogue. In activist research there is a commitment to move beyond procedural empowerment whereby research participants feel valued as part of the research process, to a focus on what Cram and Pipi (1997) describe as outcome empowerment; that is, a contribution to enduring change in social and political actions generated from the research.

In this paper we tell a part of our story as activist researchers. This part of our story is about a contribution to sustained challenges to the institutional racism that activist scholars intend to change. It is a story told in part as a simple vignette on our work, in part through the academic voice that is most often our medium of communication and, in its most important part, a call to reflection and action that will eliminate racism from our institutional procedures. We depict these elements of our work together on a paper napkin—that everyday object produced from the fruits of earth and the labour of many—an every-

---

1 Aotearoa is one of the original Māori names for New Zealand.
2 The indigenous people of Aotearoa.

day object that we so often dispose of in the unthinking manner in which we conduct so much of our everyday, taken-for-granted lives.

Locating our work

We are two Pākehā (settler) activist and critical management scholars with feminist orientations. We are interested in enhancing social justice and equity in the world and in advancing the interests of Mother Earth. We have long-standing commitments to maintaining honourable relationships and alliances with indigenous peoples. In New Zealand, the country we call home, Te Tiriti o Waitangi[3] (1840) is the treaty negotiated between hapū (sub-tribes) and the British Crown[4] which defined the terms of conditions of British governance and subsequent acceleration of settlement. Te Tiriti reaffirmed Māori sovereignty as recognised in He Wakaputunga o Te Rangatiratanga o Nu Tireni (The Declaration of Independence of 1835) and guaranteed Māori equal citizenship rights with those British ideas under development at that time. Breaches of Te Tiriti by the settler government have been documented within Waitangi Tribunal reports[5] tracing back to within months of the treaty signing (Waitangi Tribunal, 1986, 1996, 1998; Williams, 2001). Came (2013a:77) maintains 'Pākehā political, economic, ideological hegemony was systematically established by force, by parliament, by democracy and the everyday workings of kāwantanga' [governorship].

Since 1840 Māori land has been alienated, Māori language has been marginalised, and Māori legal, health and education systems have been diminished. These have been supplanted with mono-cultural systems of law and order imported from Britain (Huygens, Murphy and Healy, 2012). These systems are now under increasing pressure from the homogenising influences of a globalising health industry that morphs all humans into consumers of products and services devised to maximise the profit and power of a global elite (Biehl and Petryna, 2013). Many argue the impact of the intergenerational legacy of this violence is reflected in enduring inequities in health, social and educational outcomes between Māori and non-Māori (Ministry of Social Development, 2010, Robson and Harris, 2007). The trajectory of a homogenised global health

---

3 Within this text we are deliberately referring to the Māori text of Te Tiriti o Waitangi instead of the English version as this was the text that was signed on 6 February by Hobson and the overwhelming majority of Māori rangatira (chiefs). It is also the text of the Treaty recognised within international law.

4 The force invoked to discipline various unrest brought about by European settler disruptions to this land, but later harnessed to the land-grabbing interests of the later settlers.

5 The Waitangi Tribunal is a permanent independent commission of enquiry charged with investigating and making recommendation on claims brought by Māori related to policies, practices or omissions of Crown Ministers and officials that allegedly breached either of the Māori text of Te Tiriti o Waitangi or the English version.

industry (despite its explicit rhetoric to respect diversity in its pursuit of profit) does not bode well for the wellbeing of indigenous peoples the world over (Department of Economic and Social Affairs, 2009). This observation should serve as a sober warning perhaps for us all. It is from a context of past injustice and ongoing harm that we write about the contemporary institutional racism within the New Zealand public sector and more specifically the public health sector.[6]

Institutional racism

Institutional racism is complex and multi-layered. It is a pattern of differential access to material resources and power determined by race which advantages or privileges one sector of the population while disadvantaging or discriminating against another (Came, 2013a). It can present as both action and inaction. It is difficult to detect by those for whom the attributes of privilege shroud their perceptions of justice. As privileged people we tell ourselves that we are a just people—and we wish to believe it. As privileged people, we have many opportunities to speak out against routinised discrimination and degradation of people and planet. These opportunities are brought about by the privileges generated from being Pākehā (settler) in a world that favours this way of being. Opportunities to speak out are often forgone or not sustained over time. We as authors count ourselves among those people for whom acute attention to the opportunities and responsibilities of our privilege is sporadic at best. We seek to contribute to a change in this situation. To do so, we need tenacity of intent and practice, and a thick skin to resist the discipline of the associated social discomfort that comes with the calling to attention of the impact of our privileges.

It is challenging to draw continuous attention to our daily cavalier treatment of each other and of Mother Earth. We draw a parallel lesson from the thoughtless use and disposal of paper napkins. Mostly we do not notice their pervasiveness in our taken-for-granted everyday lives. We might even espouse an overt commitment to environmental sustainability most of the time. It can be tiresome to be constantly reminded to notice systemic conflicts and paradoxes that go well beyond what we can personally address in this single seemingly insignificant item in the armoury of the subtle abusiveness of consumerism. We can flaunt our choice of apparently bio-friendly, recyclable products with which

---

6 Public health within this paper refers to population-based interventions to enable people to increase control over the factors that determine their health, not the provision of clinical services. The Ministry of Health has the core responsibility for overseeing policy development and funding services in this area. These services are delivered by Public Health Units working within District Health Boards, by Primary Healthcare Organisations, non-governmental organisations and, since the mid-1990s, Māori health providers. The health system is overseen by an elite group of senior managers under the direction of the Minister and Associate Ministers of Health.

we appease our conscience and numb our consciousness. It is more comfortable to not-notice our wider embroilment in a culture of consumption. All that recycling of so much stuff, however, endorses our human identity as consumers, first and foremost. Institutional racism is similarly difficult to notice, and also to not-notice once we have been made aware of its pervasiveness. But how can we make the seemingly invisible, more visible, particularly when, in the trying, we make people uncomfortable (Kirton, 1997)? How do we act on that which most prefer not to see? How do we stay at the table to remain engaged in a dialogue for change?

Lying at the master's tables

Central to critical race theory is what Solórzano and Yosso (2002) call 'master narratives'—the stories of the powerful that infuse the common sense of whole societies and underpin the everyday logic of institutions. Leonidas Donskis calls these informing stories the tiresome ideas of the world's powerful people, their vanity, their unbridled quest for attention and popularity, and their insensitivity and self-deception (Bauman and Donskis, 2013:1). Gramsci (2010/1975) calls these master narratives hegemonic discourses. He maintains that they serve to perpetuate inequitable power relations between groups of people. They keep orderly the master's house and his yard (Thomas and Humphries, 2010). Master narratives, however, are not the only story in the land. Counter-narratives (the stories of the vulnerable, the alienated and the oppressed) can be found everywhere a master narrative is in sway. These counter-narratives may draw on ancient notions with a pull to the sacred. They may be astute and sometimes mocking of the master narrative, indignant, critical, politicised, and fluid. The more violently expressed, however, the more easily these counter narratives are policed and the more readily their policing is publicly endorsed. To become involved in transforming institutional racism is to become involved in challenging the master's legitimacy. The master, however, is adept at the deflection or assimilation of any critique and profiting from it. For this, the master needs the services of colluders and collaborators. We are all vulnerable to unwittingly participating in such service.

Master narratives as expressions of power may be found in any dynamic where story serves power. Adrienne Rich (1980) in her landmark feminist text *Women and Honor: Notes on Lying* maintains that lying has become normalised within Western patriarchal society. She suggests that women often lie through silence, while men tell vast lies that are so big they are difficult to unravel and dispute. The dynamic will not be unfamiliar to any people or person who finds themselves at the table of a reasonable, generous, or indulgent master. They may be at the table as trusted family members, indulged guests, or as slightly titillating radicals invited to demonstrate the liberal indulgence of the master. The extent to which questioning the protocols of his regime is to be enjoyed, indulged, tolerated or [c]overtly punished varies—perhaps based on the perceived potential of the radical to effect real change. Regardless, even as they are indulged, or given room to speak, any radical will be under pressure to display the preferred manners of the master's table. Those who transgress the boundaries of what may pass for appropriate behaviour, polite conversation, or stimulating debate will be disciplined—subtly and kindly at first, increasingly assertively, and ultimately violently. The dynamic is everywhere to be noted where powerful interests are at play. We have focused our work on the narratives of the people who manage the master's funding regimes in the resourcing of public health services. These regimes are often framed as technical and operational discourses, and are thus perceived as instrumental, seemingly amoral processes of the distribution of such services. These narratives often appear ahistoric and apolitical in their overt expression or selectively so. Nonetheless, they carry the values and the power of the master.

It is to the senior managers of public health service providers that we have turned our research attention. Such managers may be women or men. They may be young or old. They may identify themselves with diverse cultural heritages. They remain, however, the mouthpiece of the master's narrative and they thus embed and maintain the logic of the master narrative and the power and the pain of its naturalisation. They are a pivotal link in the narrative that maintains the racial disparities which we call institutional racism, a hegemonic manifestation of privilege.

Unravelling institutional racism

> The standard ideology says that Maori/Pakeha relations in New Zealand are the best in the world, rooted as they are in the honourable adherence to the outcome of a fair fight (Nairn & McCreanor, 1991, p. 248).

This standard ideology perpetuates a lie.

> ...it doesn't matter whether you have a centre right or centre left government you still have the same racism. It just gets cloaked a bit differently (Berghan as cited in Came, 2013a, p. 290).

In Aotearoa as in other places, there are significant gaps in health outcomes and life expectancy between indigenous and non-indigenous peoples (Department of Economic and Social Affairs, 2009). King, Smith and Gracey (2009) and Gracey and King (2009) argue that within neo-colonial contexts such as New Zealand, Canada and Australia these outcomes can be linked to the ongoing impact of colonisation and institutional racism exerted against indigenous peoples. Within New Zealand in the 1980s a series of damning reports were released. Among them is the work of Berridge *et al.* (1984), Herewini, Wilson and Peri (1985), Jackson (1988), and the Ministerial Advisory Committee on a Maori Perspective on Social Welfare (1988). This well-documented exposure of an ideologically perpetuated lie pressed Heather, the lead author of this paper, into a new round of specific action. A PhD no less! She takes up the story of her research intentionally framed to expose the lie about the race relations in Aotearoa and to call us to just action. The following sections of the paper are framed as a conversation to highlight and discuss Heather's motivations and experiences.

Heather's activist research story

Heather tells: My doctoral research emerged out of ongoing dialogue with Māori and through first-hand experience of witnessing institutional racism targeting Māori (Came, 2013a). It is also informed by 20 years of Pākehā Tiriti work, which for me has been firmly grounded in feminist analysis of structural analysis and privilege (see Awatere, 1984) and complex accountabilities to Māori via Te Tiriti o Waitangi (see Huygens, 2007). My specific research questions related to how institutional racism and privilege manifest within public health policy making and funding practices in New Zealand and how it might be transformed. The methodological focus of this work was informed by engagement with Te Ara Tika framework[7] (Hudson et al., 2010) and the decolonising challenges offered by Linda Tuhiwai Smith (1999) to non-indigenous academics. The work has a strong critical race theory orientation through its focus on racism (see Ford and Airhihenbuwa, 2010) and aforementioned utilisation of master and counter narratives.

At the centre of the research was a research whānau/reference/governance group which provided cultural and political direction for the work. These Māori health leaders and a Pākehā crone acted as kaitiaki [guardian] for the project, signed off the initial proposal and made a significant ongoing contribution to the research. Their input supported the development of the research design, its structure, overall direction and the detail of the study. Members of this whānau variously continue to tautoko [support] the dissemination of this work and the ongoing activist efforts to mobilise people to challenge institutional racism. This research was also shaped by what Hale (2008) describes as horizontal dialogue with Pākehā Tiriti workers, who challenged me to make the thesis accessible to a non-academic audience (i.e. napkin sized—easy to understand).

A mixed method approach to data collection and analysis was crafted. A literature review was undertaken, supplemented by a historical analysis, from 1840 to the present day, of institutional racism as enacted by Crown Ministers and officials. This analysis was strongly influenced by Waitangi Tribunal reports and deeds of claim. To capture the Crown's master policy and funding narratives a review of Crown documents was undertaken, augmented with an interview with a senior Crown official to check the detail of Crown practice. Information sourced through official information requests also informed a quantitative analysis of investment in Māori public health.

---

7 See Came (2013b) for a Pākehā exemplar of how this Māori ethical framework was applied within this research.

Counter narratives were developed through collaborative storytelling (see Bishop, 1996) with senior Māori leaders within the public health sector and a Pākehā crone. This work was complemented by relevant literature and observational field notes from my three years working within a Māori organisation (Te Tai Tokerau MAPO Trust) that engaged in co-funding and planning with Crown agencies. Given the inflammatory nature of the initial findings, these were tested further and refined by undertaking a telephone survey of different groupings of public health providers to benchmark their respective experiences of dealing with Crown officials.

The findings of the study revealed compelling evidence of institutional racism and the failure of Crown agencies over decades to develop inclusive policy and undertake consistent funding practices within the public health sector. Moreover, it exposed both the failure of Crown agencies to detect institutional racism within their own organisation practices and the ineffectiveness of domestic and international controls to prevent such discrimination. The study culminated in the development of a multi-entry anti-racism intervention framework informed by systems theory. The framework outlines generic structural and organisational pathways to address racism and emphasises the importance of both strengthening controls and enhancing racial climate. It also offers specific remedies to address institutional racism within the context of policy making and funding practices within the public health sector in New Zealand with potential application elsewhere in the public sector. The recognition of indigenous sovereignty and the honouring of Te Tiriti o Waitangi lie at the heart of this anti-racism framework.

Thesis on a napkin

Why a napkin? The concept of 'a thesis on a napkin' emerged out of polite queries at dinner parties about what my research was about and the social pressure to be able to explain what I was doing concisely before my dinner companions lost interest. It was also a potentially creative way to address the challenge from fellow activists to ensure my work was widely accessible, a reminder that I wasn't writing exclusively for an elite academic audience. As a seasoned public health practitioner and anti-racism educator, I knew the value of a good prop for capturing and holding the attention of an audience. In the right hands such a prop can enable others to tell their own stories of how they see institutional racism operating. Pragmatically it is easier to get someone to read a napkin than to commit to reading an entire doctoral thesis and it seems text on a napkin can make people curious.

How were you able synthesis all that information? I think in becoming an activist I went through a process of what feminists (Hooks, 2000) call consciousness raising, Freire (2000/1970) calls conscientisation, and activist scholar Kirton (1997) calls attempts at 'seeing the unseen'. That is, I learnt something about how oppression, privilege and discrimination work. These learnings came out of reflecting on my own experiences of discrimination as a bisexual woman and through the active process of being guided and mentored by Māori and Pākehā

Tiriti workers to notice where power resides, how it is exercised and to question who is benefitting from that.

With an activist background I was fortunate to start this research with a strong theoretical base. This was supplemented by two decades of working in the public health sector which gave me the opportunity to witness how different groups of providers were handled by Crown officials. The wave (see Fig. 1), developed by activist priest Fanchette, shows how people see the world from different viewpoints, each of which are valid and real to them. The challenge from an activist scholarship perspective is about being able to look across all the sites of the wave and expose the discrimination and privilege inherent within systems. As Paradies (2005) argues, wherever there is a group being disadvantaged by racism there is another experiencing advantage and/or privilege as a result of that discrimination.

Figure 1 **The Wave**

Retrieved from http://awea.org.nz/sites/default/files/Wavecolfooteronly.jpg. Reprinted with permission.

Figure 1 depicts a widely utilised structural analysis tool that was introduced to Aotearoa by Father Fanchette from Martinique and was illustrated by Jenny Rankin for the Auckland Workers Education Association.[8]

Whakawhanaungatanga [relationship building] according to Royal (1998) is central to kaupapa Māori[9] approaches. I was able to negotiate access to Māori health leaders due to existing, often longstanding relationships. The storytellers within my thesis chose to tautoko (support) the kaupapa [philosophy] of the research. Indeed many of them took the extra and unusual step to agree to be identified within the research. In listening carefully and intently to these stories clear themes emerged. Whenever I tested a theme by sourcing additional information the new information confirmed and clarified the theme. The napkin (see Fig. 2) is the synthesis of the key themes from the storytelling process. It

---

8 Retrieved from: www.awea.org.nz/sites/default/files/Wavecolfooteronly.jpg.
9 Kaupapa Māori is a Māori philosophical approach where a Māori world view is considered ordinary.

contains two processes: one highlights where racism manifests in public health policy making; the other highlights where racism resides in funding practices.

Figure 2 Sites of institutional racism in public health policy making and funding practices

Source: adapted from Came 2013a

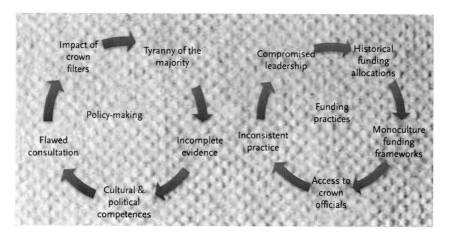

Can you explain the detail of the napkin? In relation to policy making the first site of racism is the tyranny of the majority, a reference to the work of John Stuart Mill (2006/1859). Mill argued that democracy is not a benign force; rather it serves the interests of the majority at the expense of the minority. Decision-making at board-level and within senior management teams within the health sector can and does exclude Māori priorities from the policy agenda (see Māori Policy Analyst as cited in Came, 2013a; O'Sullivan, 2003). Storyteller, Berghan (cited in Came, 2013a, 171-172) explains:

> I am the only Māori sitting around the table and there are ten of us. We are arguing the prioritisation framework and I am arguing strongly that Māori health should be right up near the top because of poor Māori health outcomes. So we have the debate…you put it on the table, you go hard for it and in the end…if you don't have the numbers, that is where the funding goes.

The second site of racism is in what evidence is included, excluded and/or misused in policy (see Kuraia as cited in Came, 2013a; Kawharu, 2001). Within the health sector there is significant reliance on bio-medical evidence at the exclusion of kaupapa Māori understandings of what strengthens health status.[10] Storyteller Senior Māori Executive (cited in Came, 2013a, 177) elaborates:

> …[we] would explain why our thinking would be in a particular direction and provide…absolute irrefutable [Māori] evidence…or talk about the necessity for tikanga for instance to be honoured… Most if not all would be soundly ignored by the District Health Board…in their white western thinking [they] were not able to give [it] any credence whatsoever… Māori thinking was not welcome at the table.

---

10 In reviewing the evidence base of Ministry public health plans and strategies over the last ten years, only a handful of Māori health academics and research institutes were cited.

The third site of racism is the cultural incompetence of the Crown policy makers who are trained in Western paradigms of health and appear to have neither the capacity nor guidance available to them to notice the mono-cultural nature of their practice (see Berghan and da Silva as cited in Came, 2013a; Maaka & Fleras, 2009). Storyteller Senior Māori Advisor (cited in Came, 2013a, 178) explains:

> …it is predominately about set values and one set of values being the norm and that is the benchmark that everything is put against. It is about systems then, that process those values and move them through into everyday working life and process them as the norm, they reinforce those views as the norm.

This cultural incompetence of some officials acting on behalf of the Crown is compounded by the fourth site of racism which is a flawed consultation process which involves asking the wrong people the wrong questions, often within the wrong timeframes (see Bradbrook and Shortland as cited in Came, 2013a; Te Tai Tokerau MAPO Trust *et al.*, 2009). Finally the policy sign-off process requires any draft policy to pass through a variety of Crown filters that frequently wash-out Māori content, sanitising policy so it is fit for the majority and will pose no political challenges (see Berghan, Māori Provider CEO and Māori Policy Analyst as cited in Came, 2013a). Storyteller Berghan (cited in Came, 2013a, 184) describes:

> What happens, as happens all the time with government policy it had to go through all the iterations, and it had to be approved by non-Māori, and because of that because of the political environment what happened was, most of it got cut out, so we got this…very safe [for the Crown] version.

In relation to funding practices the first site of racism is the historic allocations of public health funding. Sustainable funding was awarded to a range of public health providers prior to the emergence of Māori public health providers and these contracts have never been retendered to ensure they are currently held by the most appropriate provider (see Bloomfield & Logan, 2003). Furthermore mainstream providers are not monitored for their service delivery to Māori (see Senior Crown Official as cited in Came, 2013a). The second site of racism is within the service specification; that is the documents from which public health services are purchased (Ministry of Health, n.d.). These specifications are mono-cultural in their content and their structure. They marginalise Māori public health paradigms (see Te Tai Tokerau MAPO Trust *et al.*, 2009; Thomas, 2002).[11]

The third and fourth sites of racism were uncovered through benchmarking groupings of public health providers' experiences with Crown officials. Māori providers reported problematic access to Crown officials and low levels of representation on advisory and steering groups. This is consistent with a larger pattern of differential treatment of Māori health providers against other groupings of providers, in relation to contract timeframes, access to discretionary funding,

---

11 The *Public Health Service Handbook* (Ministry of Health, n.d.) for instance has a service specification for working with refugee and new migrant communities but no kaupapa Māori service specification.

levels of auditing and other elements of contracting (see Came, 2013c; Senior Māori Executive as cited in Came, 2013a; Cram & Pipi, 2001). This pattern of discrimination is entrenched through the final site of racism that is a management and quality assurance system that fails to detect and respond to institutional racism within the policy making and funding practices of the Crown.

The good news in relation to this exposure of institutional racism is that each of these sites of racism is also a potentially useful site for anti-racism interventions. Meantime the napkin serves to enable the unpacking of a complex system of racism. It also offers recipients direction about where to challenge racism. For 'good' people, this challenge is most readily made visible at a point of recognition of a paradox or contradiction in an image of ourselves as good people managing unethical systems, systems we know we ought not to engage with, systems we know we ought to wipe our hands of. It is a recognition ripe with potential. It is a recognition we ought not to turn our gaze from. Refusing to support racist institutional processes will bring us to situations in which we must act in new ways. We must call on our creativity to invent processes for the dismantling of the master's power. This is messy work. A strong napkin with succinct instruction or inspirational guidance could be handy!

Conclusion

Institutional racism is a complex and destructive phenomenon that is difficult to explain to those who have neither the eyes to see it in practice nor the moral sensitivity to feel its outcomes. Our example of institutional racism in practice is its manifestation within public health policy making and funding practices in Aotearoa. Informed by a project of collective enquiry, in this paper we have told a story of unravelling some of the ways institutional racism manifests within public health policy making and funding practices in New Zealand. It is a long story. Our telling of this story has a purpose. It is a story inviting recognition of responsibility to expose and transform institutional racism wherever it is to be found by those who have it in their capacity to do so. We have distilled it to fit onto a paper napkin or napkin-sized hand-out for ready use at many tables, conveniently sized for easy transportation by busy academics, managers and/ or activists. The key words on the napkin make for excellent conversation starters, lie detectors, and demystifiers of the everyday institutional practices that we each find ourselves embroiled in—even as we see ourselves as a just people with a desire for a more equitable outcome in the access of public health services or the other necessities and joys of human life. The napkin can be freely reproduced, elaborated, beamed up electronically or left lying about. It can be decorated in diverse styles to grace any table. We invite you to reproduce this napkin and distribute it widely. It seems a very good added use for the many paper napkins at our disposal. We invite you to discuss its contents at your next dinner party, executive lunch, or university seminar. We invite you to create your own napkins that tell stories of racist practices and ways to transform these.

References

Awatere, D. (1984). *Maori sovereignty*. (Auckland, New Zealand: Broadsheet).

Bauman, Z. & Donskis, L. (2013). *Moral Blindness: The loss of sensitivity in liquid modernity*. (Cambridge, UK: Polity).

Berridge, D., Cowan, L., Cumberland, T., Davys, A., McDowell, H., Morgan, J., Riley, L., Ruck, A., & Wallis, P. (1984). *Institutional racism in the Department of Social Welfare*. (Auckland, New Zealand: Department of Social Welfare).

Biehl, J., & Petryna, A. (2013). *When people come first: Critical studies in global health*. (Princeton, NY: Princeton University Press).

Bishop, R. (1996, June). Collaborative storytelling: Meeting indigenous peoples' desires for self-determination in research. *Proceedings of the Indigenous Education Around the World: World Indigenous People's Education Conference* (pp. 1-30). (Albuquerque, New Mexico).

Bloomfield, A., & Logan, R. (2003). Quality improvement perspective and healthcare funding decisions. *British Medical Journal, 327* (August 2003): 439-443.

Came, H. (2013a). *Institutional racism and the dynamics of privilege in public health*. (Germany: Lambert Publishing).

Came, H. (2013b). Doing research in Aotearoa: A Pākehā exemplar of applying *Te Ara Tika* ethical framework, *Kotuitui 7* (3), 1-10, doi:10.1080/1177083x.2013.841265.

Came, H. (2013c). Beginning to address institutional racism within the public health sector: Insights from a provider survey. *Keeping up to date, 38* (Autumn/Winter), 1-9.

Cram, F. (1997). Developing partnerships in research: Pākehā researchers and Māori research. *Sites: A Journal of Radical Perspectives on Culture, 35*, 44-63.

Cram, F., & Pipi, K. (2001). *Determinants of Maori provider success: provider interviews summary report (Report No. 4)*. (Wellington, New Zealand: Te Puni Kokiri).

Department of Economic and Social Affairs (ed.). (2009). *State of the world's indigenous peoples* (ST/ESA/328). (New York: United Nations, Secretariat of the Permanent Forum on Indigenous Issues).

Ford, C., & Airhihenbuwa, C. (2010). Critical race theory, race equity, and public health: Towards antiracism praxis. *American Journal of Public Health, 100*(S1), S30-S35. doi:10.2105/AJPH.2009.171058.

Freire, P. (1970). *Pedagogy of the oppressed (M. Ramos, Trans.)*. (New York: Continuum).

Gracey, M., & King, M. (2009). Indigenous health part one: determinants and disease patterns. *The Lancet, 374*(9683), 65-75. doi: 10.1016/S0140-6736(09)60914-4.

Gramsci, A. (1975). *Prison Notebooks (J Buttigieg, Trans.)* (Vol. 3). (Columbia, NY: Columbia University Press).

Hale, C. (2008). *Engaging contradictions: Theory, politics and methods of activist scholarship*. (Los Angeles, CA: University of California Press).

Herewini, M., Wilson, R., & Peri, M. (1985). *Maori Advisory Unit Report*. (Auckland, New Zealand: Department of Social Welfare).

Hooks, B. (2000). *Feminism for everybody: passionate politics*. (London: Pluto Press).

Hudson, M., Milne, M., Reynolds, P., Russell, K., & Smith, B. (2010). *Te ara tika guidelines for Māori research ethics: A framework for researchers and ethics committee members* (pp. 29). (Wellington, New Zealand: Health Research Council).

Huygens, I. (2007). *Process of Pakeha change in response to the Treaty of Waitangi* www .researchcommons.waikato.ac.nz/bitstream/10289/2589/1/thesis.pdf.txt, accessed 6 February 2013.

Huygens, I., Murphy, T., & Healy, S. (2012). *Ngāpuhi speaks*. (Whangarei, New Zealand: Network Waitangi Whangarei & Te Kawariki).

Jackson, M. (1988). *The Māori and the criminal justice system: He whaipānga hou: A new perspective*. (Wellington, New Zealand: Department of Justice).

Kawharu, M. (2001). Local Māori development and government policies. *Social Policy Journal of New Zealand*, 16 (2001): 1-16.

King, M., Smith, A., & Gracey, M. (2009). Indigenous health part two: The underlying causes of the health gap. *The Lancet*, 374(9683), 76-85. doi: 10.1016/s0140-6736(09)60827-8

Kirton, J. (1997). *Pākehā / Tauiwi: Seeing the 'unseen': Critical analysis of the links between discourse, identity, blindness and encultured racism.* (Kirikiriroa, New Zealand: Waikato Anti-racism Coalition).

Maaka, R., & Fleras, A. (2009). Mainstreaming indigeneity by indigenizing policymaking: Towards an indigenous grounded analysis framework as policy paradigm. *Indigenous Policy Journal*, 20(3) (2009): 1-21.

Mill, J. (2006). *On liberty.* (London, UK: Adamant).

Ministerial Advisory Committee on a Maori Perspective on Social Welfare. (1988). *Puao te ata tu (Day break).* (Wellington, New Zealand: Department of Social Welfare).

Ministry of Health. (n.d.). *Public health service handbook: Service specifications.* (Wellington, New Zealand: Author).

Ministry of Social Development. (2010). *The social report 2010.* (Wellington, New Zealand: Author).

Nairn, R., & McCreanor, T. (1991). Race talk and common sense: Patterns of Pakeha discourse on Maori/Pakeha relations in New Zealand. *Journal of Language and Social Psychology*, 10(4) (1991): 245-262.

O'Sullivan, D. (2003). Philosophical foundations of Maori-Crown relations in the twenty first century: Biculturalism or self determination? Paper presented at the *Australasian Political Studies Association Conference*, Hobart, Australia, 30 September – 1 October 2003.

Paradies, Y. (2005). Anti-racism and indigenous Australians. *Analyses of Social Issues and Public Policy*, 5(1), (2005): 1-28.

Rich, A. (1980). 'Women and honor: Some notes on lying (1975)', in *On lies, secrets and silence: Selected prose 1966-1978.* (London: Virago Press): 185-194.

Robson, B., & Harris, R. (2007). *Hauora: Maori standards of health 4. A study of the years 2000–2005.* (Wellington, New Zealand: Te Rōpū Rangahau Hauora a Eru Pōmare).

Royal, C. (1998). Te ao marama—A research paradigm *Proceedings of Te Oru Rangahau, Maori Research & Development Conference.* (Palmerston North, New Zealand: Massey University, Māori Studies Department): 78:87.

Smith, L. (1999). *Decolonizing methodologies: Research and indigenous peoples.* (Dunedin, New Zealand: University of Otago Press).

Solorzano, D. G., & Yosso, T. J. (2002). Critical race methodology: Counter-storytelling as an analytical framework for education research. *Qualitative Inquiry*, 8(1), (2002) 23-44.

Te Tai Tokerau MAPO Trust, Te Hauora o te Hiku o te Ika, Ngati Hine Health Trust, Whakawhiti Ora Pai, Ki A Ora Ngatiwai, & Te Runanga o te Rarawa. (2009). *Collective submission: Public health service specification review.* (Northland, New Zealand: Author).

Thomas, D. (2002). Evaluating the cultural appropriateness of service delivery in multi-ethnic communities. *Evaluation Journal of Australasia* 2(2) (December 2002): 50-56.

Thomas, A., & Humphries, M.T. (2010). 'Raising One's Voice to the Insistent Hand of Neo-colonialism', *Ninth International Conference of International Society for Third Sector Research* (ISTR) Istanbul, 7–10 July.

Waitangi Tribunal. (1986). *Te Reo Maori claim* [WAI 11] (Wellington, New Zealand: Author).

Waitangi Tribunal. (1996). *The Taranaki report: Kaupapa tuatahi [WAI 143]* (Wellington, New Zealand: Author).

Waitangi Tribunal. (1998). *Te Whanau o Waipareira report* [WAI 414] (Wellington, New Zealand: Author)

Williams, D. (2001). *Crown policy affecting Maori knowledge systems and cultural practices* (WAI 262) (Wellington, New Zealand: Waitangi Tribunal).

JCC 54 *June 2014* © Greenleaf Publishing 2014

Storytelling beyond the Academy

Exploring Roles, Responsibilities and Regulations in the Open Access Dissemination of Research Outputs and Visual Data

Dawn Mannay
Cardiff University, UK

In the last decade there has been a movement towards facilitating Open Access to academic outputs via the World Wide Web. This movement has been characterised as one that embodies corporate citizenship because such sharing has the potential to benefit all stakeholders: academics, policy makers, charitable sectors and the wider public. In the UK, the Economic and Social Research Council are implementing Open Access compliance guidelines for research that they fund, which is interpreted by individual institutions in their school regulations. In the case of doctoral theses, there is now a requirement for students to provide an electronic format of their final work to be included in their school's online digital repository. In a number of UK institutions, University Awards and Progress Committees will only consider awarding the doctoral degree once these requirements have been satisfied. Although this move to Open Access can be considered as an egalitarian endeavour, this paper argues that an important stakeholder may have been overlooked in the march towards progressive dissemination. The temporal space between gaining informed consent from research participants and the changing nature of the accessibility of outputs can both engender a breach of ethics in terms of the initial agreements negotiated with participants and raise issues around representation in the ongoing dissemination and reformulation of the original work, particularly where visual images are central to research outputs. The paper utilises autoethnography and poetry to reflect on my own encounter with the requirement for Open Access and the ways in which this brings up concerns around ethics, obligations and integrity.

- Anonymity
- Autoethnography
- Corporate citizenship
- Ethics
- Higher education
- Informed consent
- Open Access
- Poetry
- University regulations
- Visual methods

Dr **Dawn Mannay** is a Lecturer in Social Science (Psychology) at Cardiff University and also held the posts of Associate Lecturer at the Open University in Wales and Visiting Lecturer at the University of Newport, as well as being involved with the Women Making a Difference Programme. Her research interests revolve around class, education, gender, geography, generation, national identity, violence and inequality and she employs participatory, visual, creative and narrative methods in her work with communities.

Cardiff University, School of Social Sciences, Room 103, Glamorgan Building, King Edward VII Avenue, Cardiff CF10 3WT, UK

MannayDI@cardiff.ac.uk

www.cardiff.ac.uk/socsi/ contactsandpeople/ academicstaff/M-P/mannay-overview.html

P EASE (2012) PRESENTS ACADEMIC WRITING as a form of activism and political practice that has the ability to motivate and compel the reader to take action against injustice and challenges the researcher to move beyond the dense, dry, flat prose that form a 'linguistic armor' (Lerum, 2001). When we are writing as a project of social justice, then, it is important to engage both cognitively and emotionally with an audience. The call for papers for this special issue of *The Journal of Corporate Citizenship* specifically asked writers to engage in 'storytelling beyond the academic article', which would be accessible, interesting and useful. For these reasons there follows an autoethnographic poem focusing on the need to consider all stakeholders in the march towards progressive dissemination; this alternative form of presentation aims to bring the issues of corporate citizenship discussed in the following sections to life and emphasise the need for caution in the charge towards Open Access.

It's nice to share
This is what we tell our children
Don't be selfish
Sharing has an inherent goodness
It's good to share
Mutually beneficial dissemination
Egalitarian Open Access
Sharing is implicitly, corporate responsibility
Is this corporate citizenship?

It's not nice to steal
This is what we tell our children
Don't be selfish
You shouldn't take what's not yours
It's bad to steal
Did you ask if you could use it?
Mutually beneficial dissemination
But informed consent?
Right to withdraw, unethical sharing
Is this corporate citizenship?

Social research is a privilege
Not a right
We are placed in a position
One of trust
Informed consent acts as a promise
Participants generously share their stories
Their experiences
Their subjectivities
Their lives
Authors and owners

Social researchers are offered
An insight

For which they offer assurances
Informed consent
Researchers listen and interpret
Participants' experiences
Participants' subjectivities
Participants' lives
Authors and owners?

Informed consent offers an ethical foundation
It is the anchor to promises made
Perhaps the sea of World Wide Web dissemination
Offers new opportunities
The greater good
A global and accessible representation of knowledge
Compelling or
Controlling and
Compromising

Open Access is an egalitarian endeavour
But not all data has been granted access
Participants' voices; particularly the marginalised
Have traditionally been neglected in academia
Contemporary research demands change
Participatory practices and projects of social justice
Open Access then should never override informed consent
If this is lost and forgotten in the rush towards Open Access
Researchers need to put on the brakes
Rock the boat of new conventions
Consider what is right, agreed, informed
This is corporate citizenship

Contextualisation

The Berlin Declaration on Open Access to Knowledge in the Sciences and Humanities (2003) set out a vision of a global and accessible representation of knowledge. This vision was to be facilitated by encouraging researchers and grant recipients to support Open Access by providing their resources on the internet according to the principles of the Open Access paradigm, a mission of disseminating research to constitute a global and interactive representation of human knowledge and the guarantee of worldwide access. The unfolding of this vision can be seen in contemporary Open Access literature, which is composed of online copies of a number of research outputs such as peer-reviewed journal articles and conference papers, reports, working papers and theses. In most cases licensing restrictions do not apply to Open Access literature and it can be used freely for research, teaching and other purposes. This knowledge is accessed through archives or repositories that are digital collections of research articles that have been placed there by their authors located in universities or other research-based institutions.

By 2006 there were 77 Open Access UK-based archives and several of the UK Research Councils required their grant-holders to deposit a copy of any publications resulting from the research they fund in an appropriate Open Access repository as soon as possible after publication (Hassen 2006). More recently, the Research Councils UK Policy on Access to Research (2012) has provided a set of Open Access requirements for all outputs published after 1 April 2013; although it suggests earlier compliance is preferable. The policy also discusses extending existing mechanisms to include compliance monitoring for this policy as well as to track the shift to Open Access and the anticipated changes for the wider academic and political community. In this way compliance with unrestricted, online access to peer-reviewed and published scholarly research papers becomes a proviso of securing research funding.

True corporate citizenship involves far more than what has traditionally been called corporate social responsibility because, as Waddock (2003: 3) maintains, corporate citizenship requires developing mutually beneficial, interactive and trusting relationships between the company and its many stakeholders— employees, customers, communities, suppliers, governments, investors and the third sector. This conception of corporate citizenship is necessarily achieved through the implementation of the company's strategies and operating practices. However, in the move toward Open Access there is a danger that the interests of one set of stakeholders, namely research participants, could be overlooked; an imbalance which could unintentionally elevate particular institutional interests 'above broader values of community and corporate citizenship' (Swanson and Frederick, 2003: 25).

Being a good corporate citizen means treating all stakeholders with dignity and respect, being aware of the company's impacts on stakeholders and 'working collaboratively with them when appropriate to achieve mutually desired results' (Waddock, 2003: 3). In the university research setting, collaboration between the researcher and the researched should be premised upon a strong ethical foundation. As Cocks (2006) argues, issues of power relationships in research are part of the ethical maze facing researchers but ensuring that ethical guidelines are followed, such as the right to withdraw and informed consent, provides some directions with which to map the maze. However, arguably the frameworks set out by ethics boards have become in some ways a piecemeal, tick-box exercise and researchers need to take responsibilities not simply for research ethics but for research etiquette.

Research inquiry is always a moral enterprise, but when we apply qualitative methods ethical issues can be amplified not least because the researcher is delving into people's private lives with the intention of placing a version of these accounts in a public arena (Kvale and Brinkman, 2009). Informed consent then needs to be 'informed' and if participants agree to particular forms of wider dissemination then it is in these agreed arenas alone that their stories can be ethically shared. Therefore, in terms of a doctoral study where participants have agreed, perhaps, to have their data presented at conferences, published in journal articles that draw on fragments of the completed study and for the entirety of the thesis to be held in the University library, how then should the doctoral student negotiate the new premise that recommendations for a doctoral award are made following confirmation that the final version of the thesis has been uploaded into the digital repository? And why is negotiation, and sometimes resistance, necessary?

The Open Access argument then is presented as an ethical one: all knowledge should be freely available to everybody. This view, often phrased in all-or nothing idealistic terms has been taken up by governments with the added argument that publicly funded work should be available to any interested reader, anywhere (Wickham and Vincent, 2013); however, pre-Open Access, this is often not the wording of the participant consent form—but does this matter? Many of the associated difficulties come with the idea of informed consent as a finite agreement, where the name in the box means that permission is granted. In this conception an interviewee's consent need not be specified for Open Access, as well as the already existing forms of publication, because their consent, the signature, allows the researcher carte blanche. The signature is often hastily scribbled without a full reading of the consent form and, in such cases, there may be signed consent—but we should not deceive ourselves that such consent is in any way informed or ethical.

In visual social science research there have been calls for informed consent to be reconceptualised as something that is not fixed but fluid so that the use of images and interview data is continually negotiated with research participants; such participatory practice aims to rebalance the issue of unequal power in the research relationship (Wiles et al., 2008). There have also been innovative alternatives to the standard consent form where digital podcasts are employed to keep the attention of participants and ensure that they are fully informed about to what exactly they are consenting (Hammond and Cooper, 2011). As a visual researcher, I was guided by this discourse of negotiated ethical responsibility and I wanted to ensure a level of fluidity and consent that was fully informed; a particular challenge when participant groups come from outside the academy and may have no experience of the forms of dissemination commonly employed within the university setting.

In response to this challenge, in gaining informed consent I was careful to take concrete examples to show participants what the unknown entity of a journal article or thesis could look like; because how can participants consent to the unknown? Where possible I also took research participants to conference sessions so that they could understand the ways in which accounts of their lives through the research would be presented to others. These visits were planned to engender informed consent. Furthermore, even when initial consent had been agreed, I negotiated the content to be presented in some journal publications, featuring both images and interview data, by asking participants to read pre-publication proofs (for example Mannay, 2010). These are the standards that I aspire to, but realistically not all research participants can attend a conference and it may not be possible to arrange pre-publication or presentation checks. Nevertheless, institutional interpretations of the Open Access movement can inadvertently act to close down the opportunity for this form of ongoing and evolving ethical relationship between researchers and the researched.

This is particularly problematic when researchers themselves are unsure about how the openness of an online repository will not only disseminate but also reformulate their original work. For example, the thesis publication form for my own research states 'Cardiff University is not under any obligation to reproduce or display the Work in the same formats or resolutions in which it was originally deposited' (Cardiff University, 2013). Arguably, whether text is in Arial or Times New Roman may not impact on meaning but visual reformatting can actively direct how an image is read. The interpretation of the audience is not necessarily the same as the narrative the image-maker wanted to communicate; indeed, it can often be markedly different (Mannay, 2010, 2013). Therefore, in the institutional regulations the initial reformat, followed by further use of the image perhaps decontextualised from the accompanying text, raises additional issues of representation.

The issue of (mis)representation can be seen commonly in media images. For example, Wright (2011) revisits the iconic print media image 'Boy Petrol Bomber, Londonderry 1969', which contains contradictory metaphors of a young boy, the innocent child, standing wearing a gas mask and holding a petrol bomb in his hand. Wright demonstrates the power of the image by charting the way that it has been canonised through its appearance in a series of murals in Northern Ireland; where each artist casts the boy differently according to their political loyalties. In this way images become signs of their times but can be reformatted to act as signs beyond their times. Thus images are reinvented and mediate new messages depending on context. It is this reinvention and the mediating of new messages that can become problematic when applied to exploring visual productions in qualitative research. It is important that the original meaning of an image does not become silenced and that in interpreting images, researchers are giving voice rather than simply voicing over. In this case then, the institutional response to the vision of Open Access threatens images produced in visual fieldwork, which can then be shaded, cropped and perhaps be employed by an individual accessing this data to represent a stereotype of particular places, people or groups, in ways that no longer represent the original creation. Importantly, the fragmentation and misquoting of textual information is also something that requires consideration.

As Bauman (1989: 163) contends, 'the organisation as a whole is an instrument to obliterate responsibility'; where documentation, guidance and institutional practices act as pressures towards conformity and uniformity that work towards diminishing individual ethical responsibility and action'; but the voice of the individual should not be extinguished in relation to the ethics of social research. In my own experience of completing a successful viva, I needed to negotiate the administrative requirement for submission of my doctoral thesis[1] to the school's online digital repository; a thesis of both words and images. In light of the issues of informed consent and representation discussed, I refused

1 Funding: The doctoral research project from which this article is drawn, titled 'Mothers and Daughters on the Margins: Gender, Generation and Education', was funded by the Economic and Social Research Council.

to submit an electronic copy despite the wording of the documentation and further guidance, which suggested that compliance was necessary to officially receive my doctoral award.

Therefore, considering the ethics of obedience (Bauman, 1989), I wrote and appealed against the procedure, explaining carefully that electronic access to the thesis would compromise the informed consent gained at the outset of the study, when submission to an online digital repository was not an institutional requirement. The appeal was considered and it was agreed that I would be able to submit a hard copy to the home library as initially stated in the documentation at the commencement of the study. As would be expected in a School of Social Science, my concerns about the nature of informed consent, once formulated into a considered written argument, were well received and it was noted that in future students who began their doctoral study before the recommendations to submit to the online digital repository would be provided with the option to submit in hard copy.

Ethically, then, the outcome was a happy ending for concerns around informed consent. However, as Drucker (1969: 210) suggests, the legitimacy of institutional aims is to satisfy their members but this 'is not and can never be the first task or the test of the pluralist organisations of our society. They must satisfy people outside, must serve a purpose outside, must achieve results outside'. Participants often reside outside of the academy, beyond the ivory tower and outside of research councils' conceptions of Open Access. In this case it is me, the researcher, who has had to stand up and reject the institutional requirement to submit my theses to the online digital repository in order to uphold the tenets of informed consent.

As Bauman (1989) argues, organisations work, consciously or otherwise, to eradicate unpredictable and disruptive forms of ethical resistance and to stop individual members from feeling and acting upon their moral judgements about institutional behaviour. However, this administrative experience suggests that ethical responsibility ultimately lies with the researcher; and that importantly they must have the conviction and the confidence to resist rather than implicitly accept the administrative requests of their institutions; even when they are guided by overarching ideologies that present themselves as being embedded in the values of corporate citizenship. Fortunately, the time of submission allowed me to bypass the administrative demand for Open Access; however, if participants are not told about the way in which these new requirements to 'electronically store, copy or convert the Work' (Cardiff University, 2013) can potentially transform and possibly misrepresent their visual and textual accounts, the problems discussed here will remain for new doctoral submissions.

It is essential that individual research councils and academic institutions facilitating the Open Access movement acknowledge the research participant as central in the production of research knowledge and ensure that the obligations of informed consent are at the centre of the moral enterprise of corporate citizenship. Again the academic researcher has a role to fulfil; as do university administration systems and training programmes, which need to ensure that they educate new researchers about exactly what Open Access entails. When participants are generous enough to share their stories, which are often difficult even to voice (Mannay, 2011), then they deserve to have the respect accorded to the original promises set out in the process of informed consent and researchers must ensure that this respect is upheld in the changing landscape of academic publishing and institutional administration.

References

Bauman, Z. (1989) *Modernity and the Holocaust* (Cambridge: Polity Press).

Berlin Declaration on Open Access to Knowledge in the Sciences and Humanities (2003) Berlin, 22 October 2003.

Cardiff University (2013) *Cardiff University Electronic Theses and Dissertations Publication Form* (Cardiff: Cardiff University).

Cocks, A. (2006) 'The Ethical Maze: Finding an Inclusive Path towards Gaining Children's Agreement to Research Participation', *Childhood* 13.2: 247-266.

Drucker, P. (1969) *The Age of Discontinuity* (New York: Harper & Row).

Hammond, S. P. and Cooper, N. J. (2011) 'Participant information clips: A role for digital video technologies to recruit, inform and debrief research participants and disseminate research findings', *International Journal of Social Research Methodology*, 14.4: 259-270.

Hassen, S. (ed.). (2006) Open Access: JISC Briefing Paper. (JISC: London).

Kvale, S. and Brinkman, S. (2009) *Learning the Craft of Qualitative Research Interviewing* (2nd Edition), (London: Sage).

Lerum, K. (2001) 'Subjects of Desire: Academic Armor, Intimate Ethnography and the Production of Critical Knowledge', *Qualitative Inquiry*, 7.4: 466-483.

Mannay, D. (2010) 'Making the familiar strange: Can visual research methods render the familiar setting more perceptible?', *Qualitative Research*, 10.1: 91-111.

Mannay, D. (2011) 'Taking Refuge in the Branches of a Guava Tree: the Difficulty of Retaining Consenting and Non-consenting Participants' Confidentiality as an Indigenous Researcher', *Qualitative Inquiry*, 17.10: 962-964.

Mannay, D. (2013) 'Who put that on there ... why why why?: Power games and participatory techniques of visual data production', *Visual Studies*, 28.2: 136-146.

Pease, B. (2012) 'Interrogating privileged subjectivities: reflections on writing personal accounts of privilege', in M. Livholts (ed.), *Emergent Writing Methodologies in Feminist Studies* (London: Routledge).

Research Councils UK (2012) *Policy on Access to Research* (Swindon: Research Councils UK).

Swanson, D. and Frederick, C. (2003) 'Are Business Schools Silent Partners in Corporate Crime?', *The Journal of Corporate Citizenship*, 9 (Spring 2003): 24-27.

Waddock, S. (2003) 'Making corporate citizenship real', *The Journal of Corporate Citizenship*, 9 (Spring 2003): 3-7.

Wickham, C. and Vincent, N. (2013) 'Debating open access: introduction' in C. Wickham and N. Vincent (eds.), *Debating Open Access* (London: The British Academy).

Wiles, R., Prosser, J., Bagnoli, A., Clarke, A., Davies, K., Holland, S., and Renold, E. (2008) *Visual ethics: Ethical Issues in Visual Research* (ESRC National Centre for Research Method Review Paper NCRM/011 ESRC National Centre for Research Methods, University of Southampton).

Wright, T. (2011), 'Press photography and visual rhetoric', in E. Margolis and L. Pauwels (eds.), *The Sage Handbook of Visual Research Methods* (London: Sage).

About the Journal of Corporate Citizenship

THE JOURNAL OF CORPORATE CITIZENSHIP (*JCC*) is a multidisciplinary peer-reviewed journal that focuses on integrating theory about corporate citizenship with management practice. It provides a forum in which the tensions and practical realities of making corporate citizenship real can be addressed in a reader-friendly, yet conceptually and empirically rigorous format.

JCC aims to publish *the best ideas integrating the theory and practice of corporate citizenship in a format that is readable, accessible, engaging, interesting and useful* for readers in its already wide audience in business, consultancy, government, NGOs and academia. It encourages practical, theoretically sound, and (when relevant) empirically rigorous manuscripts that address real-world implications of corporate citizenship in global and local contexts. Topics related to corporate citizenship can include (but are not limited to): corporate responsibility, stakeholder relationships, public policy, sustainability and environment, human and labour rights/ issues, governance, accountability and transparency, globalisation, small and medium-sized enterprises (SMEs) as well as multinational firms, ethics, measurement, and specific issues related to corporate citizenship, such as diversity, poverty, education, information, trust, supply chain management, and problematic or constructive corporate/human behaviours and practices.

In addition to articles linking the theory and practice of corporate citizenship, *JCC* also encourages innovative or creative submissions (for peer review). Innovative submissions can highlight issues of corporate citizenship from a critical perspective, enhance practical or conceptual understanding of corporate citizenship, or provide new insights or alternative perspectives on the realities of corporate citizenship in today's world. Innovative submissions might include: critical perspectives and controversies, photography, essays, poetry, drama, reflections, and other innovations that help bring corporate citizenship to life for management practitioners and academics alike.

JCC welcomes contributions from researchers and practitioners involved in any of the areas mentioned above. Manuscripts should be written so that they are comprehensible to an intelligent reader, avoiding jargon, formulas and extensive methodological treatises wherever possible. They should use examples and illustrations to highlight the ideas, concepts and practical implications of the ideas being presented. Theory is important and necessary; but theory—with the empirical research and conceptual work that supports theory—needs to be balanced by integration into practices to stand the tests of time and usefulness. *JCC* aims to be the premier journal to publish articles on corporate citizenship that accomplish this integration of theory and practice. We want the journal to be read as much by executives leading corporate citizenship as it is by academics seeking sound research and scholarship.

JCC appears quarterly and includes peer-reviewed papers by leading writers, with occasional reviews, case studies and think-pieces. A key feature is the 'Turning Points' section. Turning Points are commentaries, controversies, new ideas, essays and insights that aim to be provocative and engaging, raise the important issues of the day and provide observations on what is too new yet to be the subject of empirical and theoretical studies. *JCC* continues to produce occasional issues dedicated to a single theme. These have included 'Textiles, Fashion and Sustainability', 'Designing Management Education', 'Managing by Design', 'Innovative Stakeholder Engagement', 'Landmarks in the History of Corporate Citizenship', 'Is Corporate Citizenship Making a Difference?', 'The Corporate Contribution to One Planet Living in Global Peace and Security', 'Corporate Social Responsibility in Emerging Economies', 'Corporate Citizenship in Latin America' and 'Corporate Citizenship in Africa'.

EDITORS

General Editor:

Malcolm McIntosh, Asia-Pacific Centre for Sustainable Enterprise, Griffith Business School, Australia; email: jcc@griffith.edu.au.

Regional Editor:

North American Editor: Sandra Waddock, Professor of Management, Boston College, Carroll School of Management, Senior Research Fellow, Center for Corporate Citizenship, Chestnut Hill, MA 02467 USA; tel: +1 617 552 0477; fax: +1 617 552 0433; email: waddock@bc.edu

Notes for Contributors

SUBMISSIONS

All content should be submitted via online submission. For more information see the journal homepage at www.greenleaf-publishing.com/jcc.

The form gives prompts for the required information and asks authors to submit the full text of the paper, including the title, author name and author affiliation, as a Word attachment. **Abstract and keywords will be completed via the online submission and are not necessary on the attachment.**

As part of the online submission authors will be asked to tick a box to state they have read and adhere to the Greenleaf–GSE Copyright Guidelines and have permission to publish the paper, including all figures, images, etc which have been taken from other sources. It is the author's responsibility to ensure this is correct.

In order to be able to distribute papers published in Greenleaf journals, we need signed transfer of copyright from the authors. We are committed to a liberal and fair approach to copyright and accessibility, and do not restrict authors' rights to reuse their own work for personal use or in an institutional repository.

A brief autobiographical note should be supplied at the end of the paper including:

- Full name
- Affiliation
- Email address
- Full international contact details

Please supply (via online submission) an **abstract outlining the title, purpose, methodology and main findings**. It's worth considering that, as your paper will be located and read online, the quality of your abstract will determine whether readers go on to access your full paper. We recommend you place particular focus on the impact of your research on further research, practice or society. What does your paper contribute?

In addition, please provide up to **six descriptive keywords**.

FORMATTING YOUR PAPER

Headings should be short and in bold text, with a clear and consistent hierarchy.

Please identify **Notes or Endnotes** with consecutive numbers, enclosed in square brackets and listed at the end of the article.

Figures and other images should be submitted as .jpeg (.jpg) or .tif files and be of a high quality. Please number consecutively with Arabic numerals and mark clearly within the body of the text where they should be placed.

If images are not the original work of the author, it is the author's responsibility to obtain written consent from the copyright holder to them being used. Authors will be asked to confirm this is the case by ticking the box on the online submission to say they have read and understood the Greenleaf–GSE copyright policy. Images which are neither the authors' own work, nor are accompanied by such permission will not be published.

Tables should be included as part of the manuscript, with relevant captions.

Supplementary data can be appended to the article, using the form and should follow the same formatting rules as the main text.

References to other publications should be complete and in Harvard style, e.g. (Jones, 2011) for one author, (Jones and Smith, 2011) for two authors and (Jones *et al.*, 2011) for more than two authors. A full reference list should appear at the end of the paper.

- For **books**: Surname, Initials (year), *Title of Book*, Publisher, Place of publication.
  e.g. Author, J. (2011), *This is my book*, Publisher, New York, NY.
- For **book chapters**: Surname, Initials (year), "Chapter title", Editor's Surname, Initials, *Title of Book*, Publisher, Place of publication, pages (if known).
- For **journals**: Surname, Initials (year), "Title of article", *Title of Journal*, volume, number, pages.
- For **conference proceedings**: Surname, Initials (year), "Title of paper", in Surname, Initials (Ed.), Title of published proceeding which may include place and date(s) held, Publisher, Place of publication, Page numbers.
- For **newspaper articles**: Surname, Initials (year) (if an author is named), "Article title", *Newspaper*, date, pages.
- For **images**:
  Where image is from a printed source—as for books but with the page number on which the image appears.
  Where image is from an online source—Surname, Initials (year), Title, Available at, Date accessed.
  Other images—Surname, Initials (year), Title, Name of owner (person or institution) and location for viewing.

▶ **To discuss ideas for contributions**, please contact the General Editor: Malcolm McIntosh, Asia-Pacific Centre for Sustainable Enterprise, Griffith Business School, Australia; email: jcc@griffith.edu.au.

Business, Peace and Sustainable Development
CALL FOR PAPERS

OVERVIEW

BUSINESS, PEACE AND SUSTAINABLE DEVELOPMENT (*BPSD*) is a new journal by Greenleaf Publishing.

BPSD aims at understanding the relationship between business, peace and development. *Corporate Peace* is an umbrella concept that contains business, social and strategic dimensions. It is the capacity of an organization to consider peace and the reduction of violence as a component in its business strategy, and the utilisation of business resources to raise awareness and enhance peace. While research has been published on business and peace and peace through commerce, *BPSD* aims to be the first journal dedicated to mutual contribution of business and peace.

BPSD will publish papers on, but not limited to, the following topics:

- Cases of corporate peace, peace through commerce, and businesses contributing to peace and development
- Theoretical articles and models on business, peace and development
- Economic metrics on the mutual contribution of business, economy and peace
- Social impact of corporate peace
- Tools and mechanisms of corporate peace and sustainable development
- Tri-sectorial collaborations (governments, businesses and NGOs) to achieve peace
- Stakeholders' perceptions and attitudes on these subjects (e.g. motivations, barriers, attitudes)
- Measurements and comparisons of corporate peace in various firms, countries, etc.

SUBMIT YOUR PAPER

Papers of between 3,000 and 6,000 words are invited for double-blind peer review.

Notes for contributors are available at www.greenleaf-publishing.com/bpsd_contrib or contact the Editor for more information. Please note that *BPSD* is an online publication, although print issues may be produced for specific events.

PEACE DIALOGUES

Contributions are also invited for *BPSD*'s 'Peace Dialogues' section, which will publish in each issue and provide a space for viewpoints, case studies, responses to previous papers, sharing work in progress and more. Content submitted to 'Peace Dialogues' is not subject to a minimum word limit or to double-blind peer review.

CONTACT DETAILS

Editor: Dr Debbie Haski-Leventhal
Email: debbie.haski-leventhal@mgsm.edu.au

Publisher: Claire Jackson
Email: claire.jackson@greenleaf-publishing.com

www.greenleaf-publishing.com/bpsd